The Politics of Hiding, Invisibility, and Silence

What is absence? What is presence? How are these two phenomena related? Is absence merely not being present? This book examines these and other questions relating to the role of absence and presence in everyday politics. Absence and presence are used as political tools in global events and everyday life to reinforce ideas about space, society, and belonging. *The Politics of Hiding, Invisibility, and Silence* contains six empirically-focussed chapters introducing case study locations and contexts from around the world. These studies examine how particular groups' relationships with places and spaces are characterized by experiences that are neither wholly present nor wholly absent. Each author demonstrates the variety of ways in which absence and presence are *experienced*—through silence, forgetting, concealment, distance, and the virtual—and *constituted*—through visual, aural, and technological. Such accounts also raise philosophical questions about representation and belonging: what must remain absent, and what is allowed to be present? Who decides, and how? Whose voices are heard? Recognizing the complexity of these questions, *The Politics of Hiding, Invisibility, and Silence* provides a significant contribution in reconciling theorizations of absence with everyday life.

This book was originally published as a special issue of *Space & Polity*.

Rhys Dafydd Jones, Coleg Cymraeg Cenedlaethol Lecturer at Aberystwyth University, researches the geographies of religion in rural spaces.

James Philip Robinson is a cultural-historical geographer at Queen's University, Belfast, researching the geographies of camouflage.

Jennifer Turner's interdisciplinary work at the University of Leicester focuses upon prison architecture and design, and its relationship to penal purpose.

The Politics of Hiding, Invisibility, and Silence

Between Absence and Presence

Edited by
Rhys Dafydd Jones, James Philip Robinson and Jennifer Turner

Routledge
Taylor & Francis Group

LONDON AND NEW YORK

First published 2015
by Routledge
2 Park Square, Milton Park, Abingdon, Oxon, OX14 4RN, UK

and by Routledge
711 Third Avenue, New York, NY 10017, USA

Routledge is an imprint of the Taylor & Francis Group, an informa business

© 2015 Taylor & Francis

British Library Cataloguing in Publication Data
A catalogue record for this book is available from the British Library

ISBN 13: 978-1-138-83056-1

Typeset in Palatino
by RefineCatch Limited, Bungay, Suffolk

Publisher's Note
The publisher accepts responsibility for any inconsistencies that may have arisen during the conversion of this book from journal articles to book chapters, namely the possible inclusion of journal terminology.

Disclaimer
Every effort has been made to contact copyright holders for their permission to reprint material in this book. The publishers would be grateful to hear from any copyright holder who is not here acknowledged and will undertake to rectify any errors or omissions in future editions of this book.

Contents

Acknowledgements

A number of people have been central to this book, from its conceptualization to its publication (firstly as a special issue, and now as this volume). We are very grateful to all who inspired and supported us throughout this process. Colleagues at the Department of Geography and Earth Sciences, Aberystwyth University provided inspiration and relief in equal measure, and we are grateful to have experienced such a supportive and vibrant environment as doctoral students. We are thankful to all who contributed to the sessions organized at the 2011 AAG Annual Meeting in Seattle, both through the engaging papers that constitute this issue, and from stimulating questions that prompted their development. We are also indebted to Professor Ronan Paddison for his editorial guidance in developing the papers into a special issue for *Space & Polity*, to the anonymous reviewers for their helpful and insightful comments, to Stephen Thompson and Zoe Everitt at Taylor and Francis for their advice on its transformation into this volume, and to Rhona Carroll in her careful management of the project. Finally, we are grateful to our families and friends for their continued support and welcome distractions throughout this process. *Diolch o galon i chi oll*.

Rhys Dafydd Jones   James Robinson   Jennifer Turner
Aberystwyth   Belfast   Leicester

Citation Information

The chapters in this book were originally published in *Space & Polity*, volume 16, no. 3 (December 2012). When citing this material, please use the original page numbering for each article, as follows:

Chapter 1
Introduction. The Politics of Hiding, Invisibility, and Silence: Between Absence and Presence
Rhys Dafydd Jones, James Robinson and Jennifer Turner
Space & Polity, volume 16, no. 3 (December 2012) pp. 257–264

Chapter 2
A Crisis of Presence: On-line Culture and Being in the World
Vincent Miller
Space & Polity, volume 16, no. 3 (December 2012) pp. 265–285

Chapter 3
Political Presence and the Politics of Noise
Kirsi Pauliina Kallio
Space & Polity, volume 16, no. 3 (December 2012) pp. 287–302

Chapter 4
Knowing (or Not) about Katyń: The Silencing and Surfacing of Public Memory
Danielle Drozdzewski
Space & Polity, volume 16, no. 3 (December 2012) pp. 303–319

Chapter 5
Criminals with 'Community Spirit': Practising Citizenship in the Hidden World of the Prison
Jennifer Turner
Space & Polity, volume 16, no. 3 (December 2012) pp. 321–334

Chapter 6
Negotiating Absence and Presence: Rural Muslims and 'Subterranean' Sacred Spaces
Rhys Dafydd Jones
Space & Polity, volume 16, no. 3 (December 2012) pp. 335–350

CITATION INFORMATION

Chapter 7
Invisible Targets, Strengthened Morale: Static Camouflage as a 'Weapon of the Weak'
James Philip Robinson
Space & Polity, volume 16, no. 3 (December 2012) pp. 351–368

Please direct any queries you may have about the citations to
clsuk.permissions@cengage.com

Introduction. The Politics of Hiding, Invisibility, and Silence: Between Absence and Presence

RHYS DAFYDD JONES, JAMES ROBINSON and JENNIFER TURNER

In both capital-P Politics, such as spectacular world events, and the 'little-p' politics of everyday practices, absence and presence have been and continue to be particularly potent political tools, utilised to reinforce particular power relations, narratives and control over space. Absence, for example, has a long association of denying others' claim to spaces, places and participation. Whether excluding particular ethnic groups from certain residential areas (Anderson, 1987), young people from shopping centres at particular times (Staeheli and Mitchell, 2008) or homeless people from urban regeneration sites (Katz, 2001), making absent has been used as a stratagem of control that removes dissenting views and experiences from particular time/places. In short, it demarcates territory where acts, people and ideas cannot belong. Similarly, the opposing part of the binary, presence, has traditionally been used to emphasise deviance. Schivelbusch (1995) has shown how, in the development of the modern metropolises of London, Paris and Berlin, artificial illumination was used as a means to give 'presence' to misdemeanours and criminal acts which were previously concealed by shadowy and darkened spaces. For Foucault (1977), the body of the condemned served as a warning to others of the consequences of their transgressions, creating a 'spectacle of suffering' (Spierenburg, 1984). In both these cases, fixing unwanted attention on the body was a way of installing discipline both to the perpetrator and to the gazer. Both absence and presence, in this sense, have been used as methods of social control; through a mixture of writing-out and constructing a spectacle, they denote what belongs where and when: what is in place, and what is out of place (Cresswell, 1996).

However, presence ought not to be reduced to the spectacular, for the spectacular serves to emphasise extraordinary acts, not banal occurrences. It is these more banal occurrences, however, that are widely regarded as constructing 'normal' subjectivities, acts and bodies in everyday life. Billig (1995), in his seminal *Banal Nationalism*, evokes the argument that nationalism is not constructed by epic battles that give birth to the nation, but through long-term exposure to particular symbols, routines and ideas which are normalised into everyday life. Such a conceptualisation of national identity has strong parallels with Bourdieu's 'doxa' (1977), the common-sense understanding of accepted and expected norms based on the habitus. The spectacular arises, in part, from crises of doxa, where it is disrupted by acts and behaviour that are at odds with the expected and accepted. The spectacular, however, draws the gazer's attention away from the doxa and its ways of being. It is reduced to a blurred background, a contrast against which the spectacular is defined, but without being able to distinguish its residual forms precisely or in detail.

Absence is often reduced to not being present, and presence to not being absent. The papers in this Special Issue examine the ways in which absence and presence are intricately woven rather than existing as binaries: they are co-constituted and co-exist simultaneously. In this sense, they build on work on the ghostly (Maddern and Adey, 2008; Wylie, 2007) which acknowledges the interdependency of these two concepts. Places become 'haunted' through the convergence of time—past and present—at a particular site. Edensor (2008), for example, discusses the haunted landmarks he encounters on his daily commute. A former cinema is now a block of flats, but retains its distinctive aesthetics; cafés around Manchester City's former Maine Road ground are deserted, yet attest to their past capacity and business. Elsewhere, Rose and Wylie (2006, p. 475) have characterised engagements with landscape as being shaped by spatial and temporally specific "tensions between presence/absence". When the material landscape is experienced, imaginings, understandings and attachments to it are "synchronously ... [moulded by] *the absence of presence, the presence of absence*" (Wylie, 2009, p. 279; original emphasis). Traces remain, but the absence is conspicuous. This temporal aspect is etymologically referenced by the terms presence and present. Its momentary nature is acknowledged, recognising that it is not a fixture but something that has come to be and will eventually disappear (Holloway and Kneale, 2008). This temporal aspect is the foundation of the ghostly; the contributions to this Special Issue explore other ways in which the binary is collapsed.

The various ways of being present and absent are examined in this Special Issue. As we have already illustrated, there is a tendency to discuss absence and presence through the medium of the visual. The rhetoric that is widely used (in English, at least), is that of sight. This is unsurprising, considering the occularcentricity of late modernity. However, constructing the visible as present and the invisible as absent is problematic. As Beck (2011, p. 127) notes, clouds are "the visible trace[s] of an invisible atmosphere"; the absence of clouds does not mean the absence of an atmosphere or of various processes. Similarly, as Martin (2011) demonstrates, the presence of another atmospheric phenomenon—fog—destabilises pilots' 'spatial certainties' and creates difficulties as mountains, structures and other obstacles can not be identified by sight alone. Darkness also destabilises these 'spatial certainties': shadows simultaneously reveal the presence of various structures, but can also hide others, while the use of different parts of the eye during dark conditions means that the landscape is experienced differently. Colour contrasts are less important than the texture of the surface which reflects light to different degrees and can allow navigation. Despite these different ways of seeing, reducing the present to the visible and the absent to the invisible privileges one sensory experience above others. This Special Issue considers other experiences of absence, such as the distant, the virtual, the silent, the unspoken, the obscured and the hidden. By focusing on other phenomena, the papers in this Special Issue consider ways of absence that are multiple, rather than reduced to (in)visibility. Such a conceptualisation allows for exploring the ways acts, bodies and ideas may be absent in one sense, but present in another.

This Special Issue brings together six papers that were presented at the annual meeting of the Association of American Geographers in Seattle in April 2011, and formed part of two sessions which sought to bring together different theoretical conceptions of absence and presence with a whole range of empirical examples that highlighted the social, political and lived experiences of absence and presence. Specifically, the papers addressed three key questions

—How are various practices employed to conceal/silence particular groups?
—How do individuals and groups distract attention from themselves and how are absences used tactically to meet their ends?
—How do issues of absence/invisibility/silence relate to experiences, conceptualisations and the production of landscape?

Taken together, the papers that emerged from these sessions highlight implications for a number of fields including ethical governance of the Internet, regeneration and youth spaces, national identity and geopolitical imaginations, prisoner rehabilitation and integration, multicultural provision and the rural idyll, and strategic regulation and deception.

The papers in this Special Issue discuss different conceptions of absence and presence, brought about by different processes. The contributions are drawn from a range of geographical locations and at different scales, but with the theme of the everyday running throughout. Vince Miller's paper opens the collection through a discussion of the ethical issues brought about by technological innovations. The diffusion of the Internet and social networking technology into the core of everyday life and interactions has created new forms of (virtual) presence while being (physically) absent, challenging moral frameworks that are grounded in notions of proximity. In the second paper, Kirsi Kallio examines the politics of noise and voiceless political participation among the youth of Oulu, Finland. Despite the range of formal political processes open to the city's youth, she argues that their use of tactical and disruptive forms of informal participation need to be understood as a 'politics of noise' that has not been transformed into a 'politics of voice'; her paper raises questions of recognising and acknowledging political participation, particularly in regard to who and what is 'heard' and how. An oral theme is also apparent in the third paper, in which Danielle Drozdzewski deals with the unspoken and contested memory of the executions of Polish prisoners of war in Katyń. Her paper outlines how the event constituted both an absence and a presence in Polish collective memory, as discussion of it was suppressed by Soviet authorities; its selective commemoration of it in public was engineered to fit particular narratives of the Polish nation. Conversely, its place among the Polish diaspora's imagination of the homeland highlights spatial implications not only relating to diasporic proximity, but also to that of publicity and privacy. The next two papers relate to aspects of belonging through spatial presence and absence. Jennifer Turner's paper examines the way in which prisoners, through being physically and visually made-absent through being placed 'behind bars', are further denied a role in citizenship systems. The increasing emphasis placed on community-based active citizenship hinders processes of rehabilitating prisoners. Her paper examines attempts to integrate prisoners into life outside the prison, such as volunteering with the Citizens Advice Bureau, which is countered by a prison regime which emphasises the distance from the 'outside' world through regulating prisoners' interaction with it. In the fifth paper, Rhys Dafydd Jones adopts the concept of the subterranean to under-stand the negotiations made by Muslims in rural west Wales in encountering absence in their everyday lives. Accounting for 0.2 per cent of the region's popu-lation, and reliant on 'storefront' sacred spaces, they are visibly absent but phys-ically present. He argues that, rather than conforming to the usual clandestine characteristics attributed to the social underground, the negotiations of Muslims in west Wales can be better understood as a tactical making-do with resources at hand. The final paper also examines the juxtaposition between visible absence and physical presence. James Robinson examines the camouflaged land-scape of the British 'home front' during the Second World War. He argues that this dissimulationist approach constitutes a 'weapon of the weak' (Scott, 1990) that preserved the morale of the civilian population in the face of devastating air power, enabling continued contribution to the war effort, highlighting how a making-absent can be a method of self-preservation.

Collectively, these contributions highlight a number of issues that intersect with current debates about space. First, many of the case studies speak to issues about publicity and privacy. Recent work has decoupled these actions from their spaces (Staeheli, 1996; Staeheli and Mitchell, 2004, 2008), to acknowledge the different spatialities of politics. For some, disrupting these spatialities highlights acts, bodies and ideas that are 'written out' of public space; breast-feeding in public is an example of a deliberate transgression that sought to normalise it as a legiti-mate practice in public space. Such transgressions, then, can be considered as acts of citizenship to make public space more inclusive and reflexive. Similarly, those denied access to the public may make tactical use of private spaces at hand for public purposes, functioning as a 'counter-public arena' (Fraser, 1990). These con-tributions highlight a range of ways in which the politics of absence and presence are related to the politics of acknowledgment, acceptance and normalisation, skimming the surface of the public and private realms.

Secondly, physical (or virtual) presence is often seen as a requirement for belonging and participation. In his study of mosque development in Sydney, Dunn (2004) notes that many letters of objection constructed areas as absent of Muslim residents, asserting that the worshippers at facilities would be outsiders. Similarly, Woods' (2003) account of windfarm development conflicts in mid Wales identified a discourse where opponents were constructed as 'outsiders' (despite often living in the area) with an idyllised imagination of the region that is out-of-step with those of 'local' inhabitants. Such a discourse seeks to discredit par-ticular views, experiences or groups as not belonging to a place, and threatening its characteristics. In these cases, physical proximity is seen as essential in having a stake in discussion, while dissenting views are constructed as those of outsiders and subsequently excluded. Such approaches delineate belonging in a dyadic sense that ignores complex ways of belonging that straddle 'inside' and 'outside', such as propinquity (Amin, 2004). Smith (1993), for example, examines how a locally born lady who complained about the inclusion of racial archetypes in the annual carnival in Peebles in the Scottish Borders was dismissed as an out-sider who had been exposed to Edinburgh's sensitivities for too long, while both racism and multiculturalism were constructed as urban and English phenomena. At the heart of these kinds of considerations are questions about who is acknowl-edged as present and, subsequently, as belonging and having a voice. The papers in this Special Issue examine how proximity does not equate to a voice, and the different figurations of proximity and acknowledgement.

Absence and presence are evoked through a range of social and spatial processes. A particularly pertinent example is that of nation-building, where selective representations of the nation are apparent. Jones and Merriman (2009), for example, illustrate how monolingual English-language road signs erected in Wales were quotidian reminders of exclusion of the Welsh language (and, by extension, acknowledgement of the minority nationhood) from the British state. In France, the nation-building projects of 'turning peasants into Frenchmen' that commenced following the revolution but continued throughout the 19th and 20th centuries placed emphasis on consistency in republican citizenship rather than acknowledgement of difference. Particular narratives are emphasised and made present through national curricula, infrastructure programmes and art, so that the societal culture penetrates everyday life as a taken-for-granted and common-sense experience. Such making-absence is not limited to the territorial confines of the national homeland. Even among the diaspora, often popularly imagined as an emancipatory space, particular narratives and interpretations of the nation permit some interpretations, but not others. Marston (2002), for example, illustrates how the Ancient Order of Hibernians refused to allow gay and lesbian people to march in its St. Patrick's Day parade, reflecting Catholic influence in perceptions of Irishness. For many Irish émigré(e)s, who had left the Republic of Ireland—where homosexuality had only been decriminalised in 1995—for New York's more liberal and tolerant society, such exclusionary attitudes were not only out of step with their perception of the city, but more conservative than those in Ireland. Similarly, Ehrkamp (2007) notes how the Kemalite secularism of Turkey was found in its diaspora in Germany: Sunni customs were encouraged in classrooms of Turkish schools, while those of minority denominations such as Alevis were side-lined and discouraged, much as had happened in Anatolia. Such exclusionary practices, which seek to deny particular groups' representations in particular political communities, highlight implications about hospitality. Constructing others as outsiders based on perceptions of absence through distance diminishes expectations of responsibility compared with those of the present—the here and now—which places the outsider as the recipient of hospitality (Barnett, 2011). However, such understandings are largely based on notions of the stranger as 'an outsider who comes today and goes tomorrow', but not, as Simmel (1908/1971, p. 143) notes, those who 'stay tomorrow', ignoring those proximate others at the margins of citizenship. Various categories—youth, convicts and religious minorities—are constructed as outsiders within, and have to negotiate acknowledgment and recognition as such.

The contributions to this Special Issue also highlight broader concerns for the study of absence and presence. First, they raise the epistemological question of how one can know. As intimated earlier in this introduction, much attention on presence relies on visibility. Being seen is paramount in being acknowledged and recognised. It is the basis of most forms of surveillance, as being seen allows for identification and measurement. Similarly, acknowledgement of popular figures also takes visual forms, from the spectacular (statues, biopics) to the more banal (commemorative stamps, 'blue plaques' recording celebrated previous residents of houses). Other sensory ways of being present are also fairly prominent, most notably sound, but also touch (Dixon and Straughan, 2010; Paterson, 2006), suggesting that presence is an embodied experience. However, presence also rests on ontological tangibility: they must have a condition which allows them to be named and recognised as such.

Recognising absence is more difficult an operation; one that rests on the absent being conspicuous. For Sherlock Holmes in Conan Doyle's short story *Silver Blaze* (1981, p. 347), the "curious incident of the dog at night-time" was conspicuous by its absence. As the guard-dog did not bark, it was evident to Holmes that the intruder was not a stranger. Yet, absence has more nebulous characteristics in everyday life. Ghostly places and spaces keep some residual and material traces of the past; other spaces and places may not have such characteristics. Consequently, absence is constructed in the context of what is present by what ought to be present. However, constructing the absent as revealed by the present means creating a danger of overlooking events that could have happened. While 'ghost towns' such as Adamstown near Dublin are the result of housing booms which overstretched their potential (Kitchin *et al.*, 2012), other 'failed projects'—such as proposed multicultural provision or planned museum attractions (Maddern, 2008)—which did not leave 'the drawing board' are absent absences. As they never materialised, it is their presence (in archive papers or planning documents) that is conspicuous against their absence. Consequently, there is also a need to understand the processes that keep absences absent, as well as those that make absences present and presences absent.

These considerations also highlight the need for robust methodological approaches to explore absences and presences. How can absences and presences be known? What kinds of senses and phenomena are privileged in research designs? What is the best medium to record them? What are the social, political and ethical implications of absence and presence? How are absences and presences experienced and negotiated? Does anybody notice if things are absent? How can the absent be captured, without transforming its meanings and associations?

Alongside these methodological considerations, reflection is needed on the ethical issues of exploring absence and presence. As Williams (2008) illustrates, inquiry has long attributed a rhetoric that evokes senses of finding 'truth' through revealing, uncovering, delving and so forth. Such a position places the researcher parallel to the heroic labourer working for society's benefit. This is problematic not only as it emphasises the researcher as expert in contrast to other forms of knowledge, but also assumes that the groups, structures and bodies that are absent want—and ought—to become present and public. Expectations, it seems, are focused on discovery, making something 'new' knowable, measurable and mappable. However, we align with Lefebvre, who claimed that his influential *The Production of Space* (1991, p. 89) was not an attempt to understand "things in space, but space itself, with a view to unconvering the social relations embedded in it": there is value in not only examining what, where and when is absent and present, but also how it is absent and present. What kinds of processes permit things to become visible, heard, acknowledged and understood? What must remain absent, and what is allowed to be present? Who decides and how? Answering these questions is beyond the scope of the contributions to this Special Issue, but is developed from their engagement.

References

AMIN, A. (2004) Regions unbound: towards a new politics of place, *Geografiska Annaler*, 86B(1), pp. 33–44.
ANDERSON, K. (1987) The idea of Chinatown: the power and place and institutional practice in the making of a racial category, *Annals of the Association of American Geographers*, 77(4), pp. 580–598.

BARNETT, C. (2011) Ways of relating: hospitality and the acknowledgement of otherness, *Progress in Human Geography*, 29(1), pp. 5–21.

BECK, J. (2011) Signs of the sky, signs of the times: photography as double agent, *Theory, Culture & Society*, 28(7/8), pp. 123–139.

BILLIG, M. (1995) *Banal Nationalism*. London: Sage.

BOURDIEU, P. (1977) *Outline of a Theory of Practice*. Oxford: Oxford University Press.

CONAN DOYLE, A. (1981) *The Penguin Complete Sherlock Holmes*. London: Penguin.

CRESSWELL, T. (1996) *In Place/Out of Place: Geography, Ideology, and Transgression*. Minneapolis, MN: University of Minneapolis Press.

DIXON, D. and STRAUGHAN, E. (2010) Geographies of touch/touched by geography, *Geography Compass*, 4(5), pp. 449–459.

DUNN, K. M. (2004) Islam in Sydney: contesting the discourse of absence, *Australian Geographer*, 35(3), pp. 333–353.

EDENSOR, T. (2008) Mundane hauntings: commuting through the phantasmagoric working-class spaces of Manchester, England, *Cultural Geographies*, 15(5), pp. 313–333.

EHRKAMP, P. (2007) Beyond the mosque: Turkish imigrants and the practice and politics of Islam in Duisburg-Marxloh, Germany, in: C. AITCHISON, M.-P. KWAN and P. HOPKINS (Eds) *Geographies of Muslim Identities: Diaspora, Gender and Belonging*, pp. 11–28. Aldershot: Ashgate.

FOUCAULT, M. (1977) *Discipline and Punish: The Birth of the Prison*. London: Penguin Books.

FRASER, N. (1990) Rethinking the public sphere: a contribution to the critique of actually existing democracy, *Social Text*, 25(1), pp. 56–80.

HOLLOWAY, J. and KNEALE, J. (2008) Locating haunting: a ghost-hunter's guide, *Cultural Geographies*, 15(3), pp. 297–312.

JONES, R. and MERRIMAN, P. (2009) Hot, banal and everyday nationalism: bilingual road signs in Wales, *Political Geography*, 28(3), pp. 164–173.

KITCHIN, R., O'CALLAGHAN, C., BOYLE, M., GLEESON, J. and KEAVENEY, K. (2012) Placing neoliberalism: the rise and fall of Ireland's Celtic Tiger, *Environment and Planning A*, 44(6), pp. 1302–1326.

LEFEBVRE, H. (1991) *The Production of Space*. Oxford: Blackwell.

KATZ, C. (2001) Hiding the target: social reproduction in the privatized urban environment, in: C. MINCA (Ed.) *Postmodern Geography: Theory and Praxis*, pp. 93–110. Oxford: Blackwell.

MADDERN, J. F. (2008) Spectres of migration and the ghosts of Ellis Island, *Cultural Geographies*, 15(3), pp. 359–281.

MADDERN, J. F. and ADEY, P. (2008) Editorial: spectro-geographies, *Cultural Geographies*, 15(3), pp. 291–295.

MARTIN, C. (2011) Fog-bound: aerial space and the entanglements of body-*with*-world, *Environment & Planning D*, 29(3), pp. 454–468.

MARSTON, S. A. (2002) Making difference: conflict over Irish identity in the New York City St Patrick's Day parade, *Political Geography*, 21(3), pp. 373–392.

PATERSON, M. (2006) Feel the presence: technologies of touch and distance, *Environment & Planning D*, 24(5), pp. 691–708.

ROSE, M. and WYLIE, J. (2006) Guest editorial: animating landscape, *Environment & Planning D*, 24(4), pp. 475–479.

SCHIVELBUSCH, W. (1995) *Disenchanted Night: The Industrialisation of Light in the Nineteenth Century*. Berkeley, CA: University of California Press.

SCOTT, J. C. (1990) *Domination and the Arts of Resistance: Hidden Transcripts*. New Haven, CT: Yale University Press.

SIMMEL, G. (1908/1971) The stranger, in: D. N. LEVINE (Ed.) *On Individuality and Social Forms*, pp. 143–149. Chicago, IL: University of Chicago Press.

SMITH, S. (1993) Bounding the borders: claiming spaces and making place in rural Scotland, *Transactions of the Institute of British Geographers* N.S, 18(3), pp. 291–308.

SPIERENBURG, P. C. (1984) *The Spectacle of Suffering: Executions and the Evolution of Repression: From a Preindustrial Metropolis to the European Experience*. Cambridge: Cambridge University Press.

STAEHELI, L. A. (1996) Publicity, privacy, and women's political action, *Environment & Planning D*, 14(5), pp. 601–619.

STAEHELI, L. A. and MITCHELL, D. (2004) Spaces of public and private: locating politics, in: C. BARNETT and M. LOW (Eds) *Spaces of Democracy: Geographical Perspectives on Citizenship, Participation, and Representation*, pp. 147–160. London: Sage.

STAEHELI, L. A. and MITCHELL, D. (2008) *The People's Property? Power, Politics and the Public*. London: Routledge.

WILLIAMS, R. (2008) *Notes on the Underground: An Essay on Technology, Society, and the Imagination*. Cambridge, MA: MIT Press.

WOODS, M. (2003) Conflicting environmental visions of the rural: windfarm developments in mid Wales, *Sociologia Ruralis*, 43(3), pp. 271–288.

WYLIE, J. (2007) The spectral geographies of W. G. Sebald, *Cultural Geographies*, 14(2), pp. 171–188.

WYLIE, J. (2009) Landscape, absence and the geographies of love, *Transactions of the Institute of British Geographers* N.S., 34(3), pp. 275–289.

A Crisis of Presence: On-line Culture and Being in the World

VINCENT MILLER

Abstract. This paper is a discussion about presence and its relationship to ethical and moral behaviour. In particular, it problematises the notion of presence within a contemporary culture in which social life is increasingly lived and experienced through networked digital communication technologies alongside the physical presence of co-present bodies. Using the work of Heidegger, Levinas, Bauman and Turkle (among others), it is suggested that the increasing use of these technologies and our increasing presence in on-line environments challenges our tendencies to ground moral and ethical behaviours in face-to-face or materially co-present contexts. Instead, the mediated presences we can achieve amplify our cultural tendency to objectify the social world and weaken our sense of moral and ethical responsibility to others. In that sense, an important disjuncture exists between the largely liminal space of on-line interactions and the ethical sensibilities of material presence which, as these two spheres become more intensely integrated, has potential consequences for the future of an ethical social world and a civil society. The examples are used of on-line suicides, trolling and cyberbullying to illustrate these ethical disjunctures.

Introduction

"It seems as though man everywhere and always encounters only himself." (Heidegger, 1977, p. 27)

On Christmas day, 2010 Simone Back, a 42-year-old social worker in the UK shared the Facebook status update "took all my pills, be dead soon, bye bye everyone". Simone had 1082 friends on Facebook, but instead of prompting a reaction or response to this cry for help, the message provoked an on-line debate on Simone's Facebook wall. Some friends mocked and/or openly doubted the sincerity of the attempt and others suggested that previous responders would soon regret their comments if the message was, in fact, sincere. To the observers, the event was seemingly abstracted and objectified. No one called for help or attempted to contact Simone by other means, despite the fact that several friends lived within walking distance of Simone's apartment. Seventeen hours later, Simone's mother was informed of the status update via text message and police found Simone dead shortly after. Simone's mother was, of course, left baffled as to why none of her daughters' 'friends' did anything to help. In this case, connectivity did not equate to community, care or responsibility.

In a similar, but perhaps even more shocking, case a 19-year-old Floridian, Abraham Biggs, committed suicide in November 2008 live on webcam after posting his intentions on one Internet forum and his suicide note on another. Some 1500 people watched his suicide live on 'Justin.TV'. During this period, Abraham was both encouraged to commit the act and berated by several on-line spectators. After several hours of Abraham lying motionless, police were eventually called.

A year earlier, a British man hung himself live on webcam in front of 100 on-line spectators after being goaded into the act in an Internet insult chat room. It is estimated that, in the UK alone, several dozen suicides have been attributed to suicide-focused Internet chat rooms and forums, which portray suicide as a reasonable option to a wide scope of people and will even provide useful tips and instructions on technique (Slack, 2008; Hurst, 2011).

All of these incidents provoked shock and debate within the popular press and on-line media, not only because of the inaction of the witnesses involved, but also because of the cruelty on the part of some in encouraging and insulting the unfortunates involved. In the aftermath of the Simone Back incident, there were calls for Facebook to take more responsibility for the actions of its users and their on-line content. Indeed, in recent years there has been an increasing amount of concern in the popular press over how social life is being conducted on the Web and on the amount of anti-social or problematic behaviour that seems to be endemic in digital culture. Calls remain in the popular press and among the families of victims for governments to step in to regulate interpersonal behaviour on-line, despite the technical difficulties involved and a general reluctance on the part of the Internet community at large to curtail speech or increase censorship. Nonetheless, there have been renewed efforts on the part of states to regulate such behaviour, much in the same way that on-line commercial exchange and notions of 'property' have become more regulated in the past decade.

This paper is not a discussion of Internet-related suicide. The extreme and deliberately provocative examples already described are designed to demonstrate a certain moral and ethical problematic: about responsibility, about how people in contemporary (and increasingly on-line) life encounter the world and each other, and how these issues are related to geographical notions of presence, co-presence and proximity. Thus, this paper is an enquiry into the relationship between ethical behaviour and the changing nature of presence in modernity through contemporary communications technology.[1]

This is significant because the on-line sphere is still often considered (and often celebrated) as a 'liminal' space with its own set of norms and where the conventions of civil society are less apparent. However, the spaces of networked digital technologies are no longer liminal since they are now part-and-parcel of the experience of everyday life and the medium through which an increasing amount of social life is conducted. In that sense, an important disjuncture exists with potentially serious consequences for the future of an ethical social world and a civil society. I suggest that, if we desire ethical behaviour in social environments that are often technologically mediated, increasingly large in geographical extent, and dynamic in terms of our presence to one another, then these changes in presence we are experiencing demand a more thoughtful and critical understanding in terms of their implications for ethical behaviour.

I argue that the relationship between presence,[2] ethics and communications technology can be examined in two ways. First, the way we see ourselves as present in the world influences how we understand, approach and treat the world, and thus has ethical consequences. Such a statement is investigated through Heidegger's critique of metaphysical presencing, the use of technology and the resulting nihilism in modern technological life. Secondly, I will examine the relationship between ethics, responsibility and physical proximity to other people. This will be discussed largely through the work of Emmanuel Levinas and the ethics of encounter.

In terms of structure, this essay will first present an overview of recent popular and academic critiques of social life as mediated through digital networking technologies, focusing on social isolation, anti-social behaviour and attempts by states to manage interpersonal behaviour on-line. It will then briefly discuss the notion of presence and how presence is complicated by the use of information technologies. In subsequent sections, I will move on to discuss Heidegger's characterisation of Western metaphysical ways of being, his concept of Enframing, and then look at Levinas' discussion of ethical encounter and the mediation of 'face'. I conclude by suggesting that, if we desire ethical conduct within an increasingly significant on-line social sphere, we need to recognise and work against our cultural and technological tendency towards abstraction, instrumentalism and metaphysical presencing, re-examine our focus on locality in our horizons of care and strive for ways to re-establish sensual aspects of physical presence in mediated encounter.

The 'Tone of Life' On-line

> Georgina was a beautiful young girl. She will be missed dearly. It's such a shame to loose [sic] her. Everyone who knew her said she was an amazing person. To all you trolls, fuck off, you low life pieces of shit (Facebook memorial page, anonymised).

> If anybody sees a nasty comment from a troll, please just DELETE it and IGNORE it. Don't fire back! (Facebook memorial page, anonymised).

The past two years have seen the phenomenon of 'trolling' emerge into popular concern through the mainstream press as well as in legislative arenas. These two examples, taken from different memorial pages on Facebook, are indicative of the effect of the recent phenomenon of 'RIP trolling', in which pages set up to mark the death of a particular individual (usually by friends or family members) become the means to taunt these friends and family members through cruel comments about the deceased. These sometimes even involve the creation of bespoke images and video clips depicting the deceased in upsetting ways.[3] Just as in any other form of trolling, the aim of RIP trolling is to provoke reactions, cause disruption and argument, and create emotional distress for one's own enjoyment. The 2010 jailing of Sean Duffy (the second person in the UK to be jailed for trolling behaviour) for posting abusive messages on Facebook memorial sites seemed to mark the ascendency of the troll into public consciousness, at least in the UK.

In its original incarnation, trolling referred to the use of interactive features of the Web, such as comments facilities and forums to create disruption and conflict. However, the recent popularisation of the term 'troll' has meant that the term is now used very loosely to describe any form of serial abusive or anti-social behaviour on-line and tends to occur anywhere on-line content or opinions are posted: social networking sites, on-line forums of all descriptions, chat groups and blogs. 'Trolling' as a term now encompasses behaviours such as 'flaming' and 'cyberbullying'.

Flaming,[4] was the first term to describe on-line abuse of aggressive behaviour, having been present and studied since the early days of psychological research into computing behaviour. As early as 1984, Keisler *et al.* were studying the high levels of swearing, insults and name calling related to CMC settings. Indeed, Moor *et al.* (2010) found that 64.8 per cent of their sample of YouTube subscribers found flaming to be common on that site and that 5.3 per cent of those flamed for their own personal entertainment. Alonzo and Aiken (2004), in an experimental psychological study, found that 68 per cent of males and 32 per cent of females in an on-line forum wrote flames for entertainment (with 11 per cent of all comments on the forum deemed to be 'flames'). In another study, Castellà *et al.* (2000) found 'flaming' interactions to be 10 times more common in computer-mediated communication versus both face-to-face meetings and video conferencing.

'Cyberbullying' is also gaining attention within the mainstream press, especially following a number of suicides that were seen as a direct result of cyberbullying (see, for example, BBC, 2011; USA Today, 2012).[5] There have also been a number of recent academic studies on the prevalence of cyberbullying (or 'on-line harassment') especially involving school-age teens. While the reported frequencies vary greatly by study, Tokunaga (2010) suggests a general range of 20–40 per cent of school-age teenagers have experienced cyberbullying. A very recent large study in the UK found that 28 per cent of children between 11 and 16 (and 1 in 10 teachers) have been bullied through digital technologies, with text messaging and social networking sites being the main media (Beatbullying, 2012).

In terms of the overall environment of conduct on social networking, Rainie *et al.* (2012) recently investigated the social and emotional climate or 'tone of life' on social networking sites and found that, while the overall experience of these sites was positive, 25 per cent of adults and 41 per cent of teens had seen mean or cruel behaviour either 'frequently' or 'sometimes', with 69 per cent and 88 per cent respectively seeing such behaviour at least 'every once in a while'.[6] Such findings support Lanier's assertion that "Trolling is not a string of isolated incidents, but the status quo in the on-line world" (Lanier, 2010, p. 61).

Outside psychology, there has been very little research or mention of trolling, flaming, cyberbullying and on-line anti-social behaviour within the social sciences. This is despite a demonstrated public and governmental concern about such issues articulated in the popular press, which has precipitated calls for the state to control such on-line anti-social behaviour. The UK government is now considering legislation that will force on-line service providers to identify trolls so that they can be prosecuted. In the US, the states of Arizona and

Alabama have also recently passed anti-trolling legislation and a federal law on 'cyberstalking' (which can include troll-like behaviour) is under consideration.

The attempt to regulate on-line interpersonal behaviour stems largely from the popular conception that *anonymity* is primarily responsible for on-line abuse.[7] The assumption is that, if the assurance of anonymity is lifted, the tone of life within digital culture will change (for example, see Adams, 2011). This has been articulated in proposed legislation that gives states much more power to unveil otherwise-anonymous individuals. Some high-profile persons within the technology industry, such as Facebook marketing director Randi Zuckerberg and Google CEO Eric Schmidt have even followed this line, suggesting that anonymity on the Internet should be phased out in the coming years.

However, this is a simplistic assumption on at least three counts. First, this assumes that people are inherently malicious and that only the threat of being held accountable for one's actions is the reason people are not malicious all the time. Secondly, it ignores the fact that there are plenty of anonymous environments where people are very civil. For example, e-Bay, is an environment where anonymity is necessary, yet it is also an extremely civil and kind on-line environment. Thirdly, it is blind to the fact that there are plenty of nonymous on-line environments where anti-social or aggressive behaviour occurs. For example, many cyberbullying studies demonstrate that the perpetrator is known to the victim 40–50 per cent of the time (Tokunaga, 2010). Social networking sites (not withstanding purposely created false identities) are nonymous environments, as are text messages.[8] Such logic suggests that there is a need to introduce alternative theoretical accounts of how technologically mediated presence may affect ethical social conduct.[9]

A 'Wrong Turn'

The recent picture painted by media, advocacy groups and legislators of a Web plagued by trolls, flaming and cyberbullies is in fairly stark contrast to most academic work on the social life of the Internet. Certainly, early Internet research was, for the most part, optimistic, even hyperbolic, in terms of its praise of the potential for cyberspace to provide an escape from the body and social structures built around the oppression of co-present bodies. The Internet, it was suggested, would reactivate a moribund public sphere through increased access to information and the ability to provide a more reasoned and authentic dialogue between citizens (Dakroury and Birdsall, 2008; Hague and Loader, 1999). The Internet also would allow for more just and fulfilling communities built around reciprocity (Rheingold, 2000; Day, 2006; Miller and Slater, 2000; Baym, 2002), and also allow for unhindered expressions of self (Turkle, 1996; Stone, 1995).

However, recent high-profile studies have taken a more pessimistic tone, with a number of commentaries now lamenting various forms of 'wrong turns' taken by digital culture in terms of social life. These range from complaints about how the technology itself is being configured in ways that limit, rather than expand, human freedom and expression (Lanier, 2010; Morozov, 2011; Pariser, 2011; Carr, 2011), to studies that demonstrate how ubiquitous presence and constant communication are leading, ironically, to a decline in the quality of social engagement and even to increased social isolation, as a result of communications overload (Turkle, 2011; Harper, 2010; Baron, 2008).

For example, Turkle (2011), finds that the demands of an increasingly net-worked, 'always on', world creates a milieu of shared attention, where people focus less on "here and now" face-to-face interactions (i.e. the material presence of others) and are continually elsewhere, in a kind of disembodied networked presence with others. It is important to understand here that Turkle is not suggesting that people have *fewer* face-to-face interactions in digital culture. The overall empirical evidence for this is mixed. The suggestion here is that face-to-face interactions are now conducted in a more distracted or absent manner because of the continuous multitasking involved with immersion in ubiquitous digital communication technology. This is a conclusion also drawn by Kenneth Gergen (2002), who suggested that consciousness is becoming increasingly divided between the context of physical presence and the elsewhere available to us through communications technologies. He argued that this results in a loss of shared meanings as people become increasingly involved in virtual worlds not available to physically present others. In that sense, people may be physically present, but socially or attentionally absent or elsewhere.

Other more theoretical work has called for a more detailed critical understand-ing of being together digitally (Silverstone, 2003; Willson, 2012). This research questions the implications for the social of the lifting out of social relations from a physical grounding in the face-to-face social world and physical proximity, to a being together that is increasingly maintained (one cannot say 'grounded') through electronic networks and technological interfaces that are primarily focused around individual social networks. These create an experi-ence and a social presence that is largely metaphysical (in the sense of being beyond the physical, incorporeal, transcendent or abstract) alongside the physical presence of embodied everyday life, problematising the distinction between absence and presence, subject and object, self and other (also see Willson, 2012).

This questioning of the social and ethical implications of an embodied versus metaphysical mode of presence in the world on the one hand seems like a contem-porary questioning of a set of contexts that have been brought about by recent communications technologies but, in fact, similar concerns had been the focus of phenomenological and existential philosophers such as Martin Heidegger and Emmanuel Levinas since the early part of the 20th century. Such work pro-vided a powerful comment on modern, Western cultural and philosophical atti-tudes and the consequences of these attitudes through the exploration of the relationship between presence, technology, and ethics. In many respects, their work seems exceedingly relevant (yet largely unexplored)[10] when considering how the move to a technologically maintained social life may influence people's ethical and moral behaviour, or, as I suggest, exaggerate tendencies that are already inherent in modern, Western culture.

Metaphysical Presence, On-line Presence and Modern Ways of Being

While Heidegger himself never explicitly acknowledged an ethical dimension to his work, many scholars point to the implicit ethical dimension in his critique of metaphysical presence and the resulting nihilistic relationship that modern Western technological culture has with the world (Hodge, 1995; Aho, 2009). In *Being and Time* and subsequent works, Heidegger argued that the history of Western philosophy and culture has entailed a 'forgetting' of being and that this was the result of a dominant metaphysical conception of being in Western culture (often referred to as a 'metaphysics of presence'). He saw the Western mode of being as one of alienation: from nature, from the things of the world and, ultimately, from humanity itself. Thus the key element of Heidegger's project is to reconsider the notion of being by deconstructing prominent philosophical and cultural notions such as 'mind', 'subject', 'consciousness' and 'human being' and instead offer concepts such as *Dasein*[11] or 'being-in-the-world', which embeds what it is to be human outside the individual subject and within space, materiality, time and history.

For Heidegger, the roots of the metaphysical worldview begin in ancient Greece with the move from mysticism to classical philosophy. Whilst pre-Socratic thought did not objectify beings and objects by reducing them to an object or objects for a thinking subject, but tried to consider them in their phenomenality of presence or self-showing, 'Being' under Plato and Aristotle begins to be considered within the realm of subjectivity and as a transcendental subject of consciousness. This tradition holds that knowledge of the world is obtained on the basis of reason, which means two things

1. There is an orientation towards Being, which is centred around 'mind', 'psyche' or 'subject', which has the potential to be apart from the world and can thus seek a 'truth' of the world and give it meaning.
2. The things of the world are seen as objects for a thinking subject to consider. The 'ground' or meaning of objects in the world, in this view, resides in the thinking subject, which considers it as something present and with essential substantive properties, not, as the pre-Socratics thought, in their own phenomenality or unconcealment (Heidegger, 1962; White, 1996; Gumbrecht, 2004).

What we inherit from the Platonic tradition is a kind of subject-centred encountering of the world in which we see ourselves as present but separate: a firm distinction between the intellectual, immaterial or spiritual subject, and the material object—a faith in the thinking psyche and a mistrust of the material, sensual or perceptual.

This metaphysical form of being and presence becomes solidified in Western thought through the works of Descartes, who again focused the entirety of being within the concept of the transcendental subject and the thinking or rational mind. In Descartes' formulation, the only certainty is the presence of oneself to oneself. 'I think, therefore I am' separates the subject as ontologically prior to the world of objects around it.

This again entails a strong division between immaterial subject and material object. Descartes formulated what it is to be human as an abstract, self-enclosed, metaphysical, thinking individual subject, which views the other beings in the world as separate substantive objects of experience to be considered, thought about and empirically examined. As Aho summarises

> This method of radical doubt establishes the *res cogitans* as indubitable. The free, thinking 'subject' becomes the self-enclosed first ground from which 'objects' of experience are to be observed. From this standpoint, the external world comes to be understood as a system of causally determined parts. Beings are no longer experienced in terms of historically embedded social meanings and values but in terms of brute, mechanistic

causal relations that can be objectively researched, measured, and predicted based on scientific principles (Aho, 2009, p. 9).

Descartes effectively presented an understanding of being as something more
akin to "modern mathematical physics and its transcendental foundations" (Heidegger, 1962, p. 129). Thus we have a metaphysics of presence, where we understand our being and presence in the world as a presence to ourself as the subject,
and approach the world and the things in it reflectively, in relation to how *we* con-
ceive of their essential properties and can use them as objects available to us for
use.

This understanding lends itself to our experience of digital culture in two
important ways. First, the world of the Web is one that is set up to satisfy calculated human intention. We do not stumble upon things or beings on the Web as
we would stumble upon a porcupine or a rock when walking through a wood.
We do not encounter an Internet community in the same way we might happen
upon an unexpectedly enchanting village while on a road trip. The Web brings
things to us either directly by our own intention (i.e. searching for something
specific in which we are interested) or brings things to us because they have a cat-
egorical property in which we may be interested. With regard to the former point,
it is reasonable to suggest that our on-line presence is generally motivated by
specific intentions and goals: we go on-line to get something. That could be information, companionship, entertainment or the purchase of consumer goods. The
point is that there is a reason why we are there. When we search for things, we
are engaging with the (virtual) world in a particular way, which revolves
around the specific demands of a self-enclosed thinking subject. Indeed, the
work of Eli Pariser (2011) demonstrates quite forcefully how technologies of per-
sonalisation such as the Google algorithmic search facility actively work to create
an on-line world that is unique to the histories and interests of the *individual*
human being, atrophying the 'rizomatic' nature of the Web much lauded in
earlier techno-utopian discussions of the Internet such as Hamman (1996) and
Wise (1997). In this respect, there are no 'accidents' or 'happenstances' on the
Web. What we encounter is presented to us as always something potentially
useful to us, and in the very instrumental, rational, calculated, *mathematical*
manner that Heidegger describes and critiques in the figure of Descartes' *res cogitans* and the concept of a metaphysical presence.

Secondly, the on-line sphere encapsulates Descartes' formulation of thinking
subject/perceived object (or mind/body distinction) in the sense that the experience
of the Internet is much more subject-centred and transcendental, as opposed to an
encounter with the bodily or material. This is simultaneously an obvious and yet
still highly contested point. On the one hand, on-line presence is quite obviously
a 'mental' presence in comparison with off-line presence. Such assertions are
implicit, for example, in the mountain of work on 'Internet identity' and 'Internet
community' (see, for example, Turkle, 1996; Stone, 1995, with regard to early text-
based environments; or Boellstorff, 2008, for more contemporary virtual worlds;
and Rheingold, 2000, on Internet community). Here, the basic premise for the
radical nature of the Internet was purported to be that the absence of physical
bodies, cues and voices allowed one to construct asubjectivity free of such social
constraints that have their roots in the categorisation and oppression of bodies.
One could effectively write oneself into existence, project inner qualities of an
inner 'self' (or states of self) through textual descriptions and avatars, and be

judged solely on one's intellectual capacities of creativity, argumentation, intelligence and semiotic skill.[12] In this respect, networked life on-line is widely considered to be a more 'mental', disembodied life (Barney, 2004).

However, it is important to recognise, as much recent work does (for example, Hansen, 2006), that the body has not disappeared in on-line life. First of all, that would apply a strict distinction between 'on-line' and 'off-line' worlds, which clearly is not the case. This also ignores the fact that much on-line behaviour, such as purchasing goods, listening to music, gaming, dating, viewing pornography, getting medical and dietary information, has at its root the satisfaction of bodily needs and stimulation of the senses. Nonetheless, while this is recognised, it can be suggested that—despite increasingly sophisticated interfaces, connection speeds and graphical presentation of virtual environments—it is clear that (at least for the vast majority) on-line virtual environments are still relatively poverty-stricken in terms of sensual experience, especially when experienced through mobile technologies. Such environments are overwhelmingly based on vision and text; secondarily by sound. The experience of other senses (smell, touch, taste, proprioception) is minimal at best, if existent at all. Thus, 'imagination', cognitive inference and self-projection play an essential role in the experience of the on-line world, filling in the gaps left by a lack of sensory input.[13] Again, this demonstrates a certain amount of concurrence between Descartes' formulation of *res cogitans* of which Heidegger was so critical.

Technology, Enframing and Digital Revealing

> Accordingly, man's ordering attitude and behaviour display themselves first in the rise of modern physics as an exact science. Modern science's way of representing pursues and entraps nature as a calculable coherence of forces (Heidegger, 1977, p. 21).

In his subsequent works, and particularly in *The Question Concerning Technology*, Heidegger related his concerns about modern philosophy and a metaphysics of presence more directly to the human relationship with technology. In the modern era, Heidegger sees the rational, calculative manner of being indicative of metaphysical presencing as enhanced by our relationship to modern technology, which further encourages encountering the world with a calculative, instrumental eye.

Heidegger first considers the impact of the spread of technical relations in our world through a questioning of our understanding of technology itself throughout history, arriving at the point where he suggests that technology is more complicated that a simple 'means to an end' or a tool for humans to accomplish something, but that in its essence technology can be considered a 'revealing'. "Technology is no mere means", he argues, "technology is a way of revealing" (Heidegger, 1977, p. 12); therefore, "Technology comes to presence in the realm where revealing and unconcealment take place" (p. 13).

What he means by this is that technology is a way in which things are shown and made present to us. Modern technology is a revealing as well, but a particular kind of revealing:

> The revealing that rules in modern technology is a challenging which puts to nature the unreasonable demand that it supply energy that can be extracted and stored as such (Heidegger, 1977, p. 14).

Modern technology presents the world to us in such a way that nature and the world are seen as something to be 'set-upon'. Nature ceases to be something that is simply harnessed or worked with, but is transformed: aggressively challenged to prove itself as something useful and at our continual disposal. The world is viewed as and through powerful technologies unnaturally altered to become, a 'standing reserve' for our use.

By 'standing reserve', Heidegger means two things. First, that everything is seen to exist to serve our needs and that things and beings are thus robbed of their capacity or possibility to exist *outside* the use we potentially make of them. Everything attains meaning merely as a *consumable*. Secondly, because things are only seen to have a meaning in terms of utility to our needs, when that utility is exhausted they have no value at all, thus they become eminently *disposable*. Thus, in the modern technological age, beings appear in the light of disposability (Rojcewicz, 2006). For Heidegger, metaphysical presence and technological ways of being create a nihilism in which the only meaning or worth the things of the world possess is how they can be used or exploited. In that sense, objects themselves are denied even the status of being objects

> As soon as what is unconcealed no longer concerns man even as an object, but does so, rather, exclusively as a standing-reserve, and man, in the midst of objectlessness is nothing but the orderer of the standing-reserve... he comes to the point where he himself will have to be taken as standing-reserve. Meanwhile man, precisely as the one so threatened, exalts himself to the posture of lord of the earth (Heidegger, 1977, p. 27).

However, as we see, Heidegger goes one step further to suggest that such nihilism not only involves our presence to, and relation with, nature and inanimate objects, but ultimately gathers up our social relations as well. The irony is that the feeling of control we in contemporary society feel we have over nature through technology is illusory, because we ourselves are caught up in this technological way of being, a process he refers to as *Enframing*

> Enframing means the gathering together of that setting-upon which sets upon man—i.e. challenges him forth, to reveal the real, in the mode of ordering, as standing-reserve (Heidegger, 1977, p. 20).

Enframing is not only what technologically advanced humans do to the world, humanity itself is Enframed: reduced to the status of a resource (Pattinson, 2000). So Enframing is 'an all-encompassing imposition' (Rojcewicz, 2006) in which humans are potentially revealed in the same way as nature: shown for their useful, calculable functions; seen as consumables and disposables. Heidegger pointed out how this could even be seen in his day, through the increased uses of terms such as 'human resources', 'supplies' and 'reservoirs' of different labour pools.

Importantly, in modern technological society, Enframing crowds out other possible forms of revealing, so that the only way beings can exist or be present to us is through the light of calculable properties of potential use or exploitation. In this sense, the world in which we live increasingly takes on the properties of rigid technical relations that are not simply responsive to the needs of humans (as would be seen if technology were simply a means to an end), but orders the world (humans included) in a certain way, and presents it to us as a given fact (Hodge, 1995).

We can see this demonstrated in on-line culture in several ways. Again, Pariser's (2011) discussion of the power of algorithmic functions involved in websites like Google and Facebook is an interesting elucidation of Enframing in that, in the case of Google in particular, our encountering of the on-line world is personalised: filtered so that in any search action we are presented with links to objects (advertisements, web pages) that possess characteristics that are algorithmically perceived to be relevant to a set of characteristics indicative of us (gleaned from previous web behaviour). In other words, Google (or Facebook, or any similar site) reduces us to a set of measurable and calculable properties, orders these properties in terms of relevance and reveals the on-line world to us individually on this basis.

Lanier's (2010) polemic *You Are Not a Gadget* also articulates a critique that echoes the notion of Enframing. He suggests that the inherited limitations of software created in the past for specific purposes have now been 'locked in' as the architectural basis for contemporary software. As the Web has become part of everyday social life, and as people increasingly connect to each other through computers, much software as it is currently configured, is not fit for the purpose for which it is now put: conveying human communication, expression or personhood. Instead, he argues, humans are increasingly steered to communicate with each other and portray themselves through ever more reductionist models of abstraction.[14]

Lanier suggests that reductionist software architecture compels (challengesforth) people to express themselves through templates, categories and pre-formatted options (endemic to any social networking website, for example), prioritising software demands, technical efficiency and the need to collect calculable data, over personal expression. This revealing ultimately brackets the sense of personhood that one is able to achieve or experience in on-line contexts and tends to present others only as sources of fragments or ensembles of categories. The "deep meaning of personhood", he suggests, "is reduced to illusions of bits" (Lanier, 2010, p. 20). Again, this parallels Heidegger's notion of Enframing, as humans become caught up in the technical relations of which they are supposed to be the master. Far from being a human-centred means to an end, our use of digital technology begins to dictate how it is we ourselves can be revealed, ultimately transforming the nature of human relations themselves. This can be seen in Sherry Turkle's latest work, *Alone Together*, where such concerns regarding technologically mediated human relationships are reproduced

> Networked, we are together but so lessened are our expectations of each other that we can feel utterly alone. There is the risk that we come to see each other as objects to be accessed—and only for the parts we find useful, comforting, or amusing (Turkle, 2011, p. 154).

She argues that people are increasingly using networking technology to maintain useful instrumental connections to others. However, despite the apparent convenience of technologies that allow us to maintain a much larger and wider set of social relationships and interactions than ever before, her research suggests that we have become overwhelmed with the amount of communication (and thus social obligations) we are tied into through these technologies. The result has been a pressure to be ever more efficient in our exchanges with others and thus rely even more on networked connections to stand in and moderate our interactions with other people. Thus, technologies (in the name of instrumental efficiency) are increasingly used to keep an emotional distance and avoid intimacy (or indeed, awkwardness) with others in everyday interactions. Again, recalling Heidegger, the technologies that were supposed to help take command of our relationships with others have instead 'set upon' these relationships

> It's also that I don't want to talk to people now. I don't want to be interrupted. I think I should want to, it would be nice, but it is easier to deal with people on my Blackberry (interview data; from Turkle, 2011, p. 203).

In short, Turkle argues that we end up expecting more from technology and less from each other in terms of social interactions. Indeed, Turkle is not the only one to have demonstrated empirically how the demands for ubiquity involved in a networked presence affect communications between individuals. Licoppe and Smoreda (2005) and Grinter and Eldridge (2001) also found a correlation between technologically connected presence and a rise of compressed forms of communication that avoid social interaction or dialogue in the name of efficiency.

These lessened expectations manifest themselves in the everyday mendacity of on-line life, where this tendency to take a convenient instrumental distance in digital communications, leads to behaviour which, in many respects, can be seen as 'anti-social' because their whole sphere of conduct seems to be towards avoiding the encounter of others as beings that are a part of the world in their own right. This way of being instead sees any kind of unpredicted, unscripted two-way communication as excessively demanding, awkward, inconvenient or inefficient. Thus, telephone conversations are avoided in favour of texts, the intricacies of romantic relationships (such as break-ups) are increasingly mediated through technologies as an avoidance tactic, and an increased indifference to the sensitivity of others means that arguments, disagreements and abuse escalate in on-line environments far more quickly and more intensely than they would off-line (Turkle, 2011).

Groundlessness, Proximity, and Ethics

> There is a contrast here between being human as a metaphysical, generalised abstraction and as an ethical, located, lived relation (Aho, 2009, p. 112)

One can point out two major ethical concerns that result from Heidegger's assessment of modern forms of presence. First, he suggests that life, when subordinated to reason under metaphysical presence, becomes "technical and monstrous" (Aho, 2009, p. 16). The previous section suggested that, once the world is given over to the purely calculable, it ceases to have any meaning other than the purely instrumental and useful: a nihilist position. The Enframing, which is part-and-parcel of modern technological ways of being, parlays this instrumental, calculative existence inherent in the metaphysics of presence to new heights, gathering up all beings in the world (including humans) in a context where the only possible way that they can be revealed is as a calculable resource or standing-reserve.

The quote by Aho points out another aspect in the relationship between presence and ethics: the idea that ethics has a location. Aho draws from Heidegger the assertion that an abstract, metaphysical subject has a different ethical relationship to the world from one that is embodied, located and grounded in place. The location of the metaphysical modern subject is decidedly *unlocated* in that it occupies a position in which we have a relation as subjects to the world of objects, and yet remain aside or estranged from the world. As Aho (2009) suggests, this gives modern technological subjects a limitless domain, generating a groundlessness and a homelessness in which it becomes difficult for humans to make any meaningful connections to any location.

There is, however, a much more straightforward discussion that follows from this assertion—namely, the question of whether it matters where people 'are' in terms of their ethical behaviour. In contemporary times, this becomes important to consider given that physical and social presence have become decoupled as a result of the use of digital communications technologies. However, despite its contemporary relevance, the locatedness of ethics is, in itself, an old question.

Aristotle, in *The Nicomachean Ethics*, contrasted 'natural justice', a universal abstract notion of justice and ethical behaviour that is applicable to all times and all places, with conventional justice, which was based in localised, legal and practical circumstances. He suggested that universal notions of justice and ethical behaviour gave way to particular legal and practical regimes tied to space. Aristotle also identified that proximity breeds familiarity and a sympathy for the other through identification. Thus he stated that 'sufferings are pitiable when they appear to be close at hand' (Aristotle, *Rhetoric*: 227–228 (2.8.1386a). Thus pity (used here akin to 'sympathy') is constrained by both space and time.

In the 18th century, Adam Smith, in *The Theory of Moral Sentiments*, noted that the presence of others is indispensible in moral behaviour, as we need the 'mirror' afforded to us by the eyes of others to gain a certain reflective capacity with regard to our own actions. Seeing the eyes of others and, really, seeing ourselves reflected in the eyes of others as a mirroring gaze, for Smith, is the only way we can scrutinise our own conduct. Without this 'looking glass' of the gaze involved with the presence of others, we risk becoming overselfish (Smith, 1759/1976; Paganelli, 2010).

Yet it is the 20th-century ethical philosopher Emmanuel Levinas (1969; Levinas and Nemo, 1985) who has perhaps gone furthest in developing the argument that ethical behaviour is born out of the concrete, embodied situation of person-to-person contact and not abstract or universal principles. Similarly to Heidegger, he sees the contemplation of the object as a part of a general forgetting of being within modern culture, but as a post-holocaust philosopher, Levinas critiqued Heidegger by arguing that *ethics*, and not *knowledge of being*, should be the primary concern of philosophy, and thus explicitly tied ethics and being (Manning and Sheffler, 1993),.

Levinas does this by placing the face-to-face encounter with another person, and not an encounter with the world, as the first and primary human encounter. It is this intersubjective encounter, inevitably an *ethical* encounter, which, for Levinas, is constitutive of the subject. It is constitutive of the subject in that (similarly to Adam Smith), Levinas suggests that being is located in the focus of the other's gaze. That gaze in itself indicates that one has a presence in the world with others who are *fundamentally different* from oneself. This difference is encapsulated in the concept of 'Other' because Levinas characterises the Other as fundamentally unknowable and infinite, something that escapes any attempt at containment or categorisation available to the subject. For Levinas, our being is constituted in this encounter with something that cannot be reduced, contained or fully comprehended. In many ways, the encounter with the other is an encounter with something greater than oneself. Such an encounter interrupts our consciousness by making us realise that we are not alone, that we share the world and that our freedoms are thus limited (Manning and Sheffler, 1993; Davis, 1996).

Thus, the face-to-face encounter with the other is, for Levinas, constitutive of human existence, but this existence is also tied to an ethical responsibility for that other. It is a fundamentally ethical encounter because the physical presence of the other through 'face' addresses or calls the subject … makes demands of it

> One can say that the face is not 'seen'. It is what cannot become a content which your thought would entail; it is uncontrollable, it leads you to beyond … but the relation to the face is straightaway ethical. The face is what one cannot kill (Levinas, 1985, p. 87).

For Levinas, 'face' itself is transcendent, but it is ultimately tied to the presence of the bodily face, focused on 'the face' itself and the eyes, but also inclusive of the body as part of 'face' more generally. The face is the exteriority of the other and separates humans from the world of objects, and Levinas sees the face as signifying an order of responsibility for the other in the subject, not in the sense of a reciprocal responsibility (as in I feel that the other is responsible for me as well), but an unconditional one on the part of the subject

> The first word of the face is 'thou shalt not kill'. It is an order. There is a commandment in the appearance of the face, as if a master spoke to me (Levinas and Nemo, 1985, p. 89).

> I analyse the interhuman relationship as if, in proximity with the Other— beyond the image I make of myself of the other man—his face, the expressive in the Other (and the whole human body is in this sense more or less face), were that *ordains* me to serve him (Levinas and Nemo 1985: 97

In this respect, this encounter, the face-to-face encounter, is the very foundation of sociality (Bergo 1999). Again, this encounter is ethical because the concrete, embodied nature of person-to-person contact comes with a choice: we can either accept this responsibility for the other or be violent towards them. Thus, it is this proximal, embedded encounter, not abstract contemplation, which inherently and necessarily creates the possibility for ethics. In short, faces matter; being together matters.

Mediated Presence and the Other

So what happens when we are not together? How do we encounter others when they are not physically present but present through media? This is an important question given that modernity and modern communications technology have not only brought expanded spatial relations, but have exposed us to people and worlds of which we would otherwise have no knowledge. As Silverstone (2002) suggested, through electronic media, others have a constant presence in our everyday lives, but how they appear to us, and how we encounter them, are moral and ethical questions that have been rarely asked.

Those who have asked these questions have usually been concerned with the relationship between the depiction of calamities and the suffering of others in far-away lands, and audiences who experience such events through broadcast television (for examples, see Chouliaraki, 2008; Boltanski, 1999; Figenschou, 2011; Smelik, 2010). Being "a spectator of calamities taking place in another country" Sontag (2003) writes, "is a quintessential modern experience" (Sontag, 2003, p. 16; quoted in Figenschou, 2011, p. 235), yet in the main, such experiences have little impact on the majority of viewers. The question here then becomes one of how people are ethically positioned with regard to the mediated suffering of others. The general answer here seems to be as 'spectator', in that one is 'present to' the suffering, but not 'present with' the suffering ... it can be ignored, rejected or turned off. Through the broadcast screen, we are exposed to, but insulated from, the *actual* suffering (Smelik, 2010; Boltanski, 1999).

Within this literature, the phrase 'compassion fatigue' (Moeller, 1999) is used to describe the prevailing indifference to such mediated experiences of suffering, where overexposure to such stimulus, combined with the feeling of an inability to have an impact or influence on the suffering, creates a distance between the suffering and the spectator. As a result, there is a strong hierarchical disposition towards proximity in mediated suffering, and horizons of care in mediated suffering still have a strong bias towards one's locality and nation, as opposed to the global or cosmopolitan outlook possible through media (Chouliaraki, 2008). Boltanski (1999) thus suggests that we suffer from a 'crisis of pity' when it comes to the suffering of distant others.

For Bauman (1993), the lack of an embodied presence is a fundamental difference between strangers in the city and strangers on the screen.[15] Recalling Levinas, he argues that strangers in the city demand a response because of their physical and material presence. They need to be acknowledged and dealt with, and thus one is, as Levinas suggested, forced to make a choice: help, flee, or perhaps be violent.

By contrast, strangers on the screen lose their embodied presence and in doing so they lose their substance and moral integrity, becoming mere disembodied, aestheticised *surfaces* and thus are open to be experienced as "objects of enjoyment" with "no strings attached" (Bauman, 1993, p. 178; Tester, 2001). Telemediated strangers therefore lack a presence that has substance. They only present aesthetics and thus can be denied a moral compulsion and can be encountered in purely instrumental terms. They can be switched off if upsetting, ignored or enjoyed. Silverstone (2006) similarly suggested that the mediated other's moral presence is overdetermined by their physical absence. In that respect, the mediated face is optional; it makes no demands upon us because we have the power to switch it off and withdraw.

While broadcasting is said to give a sense of distant presence that one might associate with a spectator position, socially networked digital media, through their fundamental condition of interactivity and connectedness, are said to provide a more 'direct' encounter with others: no broadcasters, no governments, thus very few intermediaries between persons. This provides a potential closeness and an intimacy, which can generate a proximity that can overcome that spectator position where we are potentially more 'present with' than 'present to' others, and thus can expand our horizons of care beyond the local and the particular to encompass the mediated both near and far (Smith 2000). This would lead to heightened capacities of intimacy, understanding, the finding of common ground, the formation of attachments and communities among strangers and the physically absent in a way not possible with broadcast media.

Silverstone (2003) and Orgad (2007), however, explicitly question the assumption within much current work on on-line relationships that such technological capabilities naturally lead on to enhanced capacities for moral and ethical behaviour. Both authors point out that 'connectedness' may breed forms of intimacy and closeness, but that this does not necessarily lead to a greater sense of responsibility, morality or recognition. This is seen in the work of Turkle (2011), Baron (2008) and Harper (2010). All demonstrate how social isolation can be considered endemic to contemporary experiences of social connectedness through networked digital technologies. Similarly, both Silverstone (2003) and Orgad (2007) suggest that the large body of work conceptualising 'digital community' derives in the main from a narcissistic discourse of the self and relationships built around the instrumental needs of the self. This is demonstrated in the use of terms such as 'personal community', 'network' and 'the community of me'. Such conceptualisations of 'community' have no basis in a disposition or responsibility towards others or the Other, but, at best, rely on a premise of mutual instrumentalism through notions of 'reciprocity' and 'exchange', which are easily problematised through critical analysis.

For example, Orgad's (2005) empirical work on on-line communities of breast cancer sufferers demonstrated that camaraderie and care on these sites were based on reciprocity, as opposed to responsibility. Those within these communities who disagreed with prevailing views, or who had little to offer, were often rejected or marginalised. Such findings put into question the idea that 'sharing' on-line, even in seemingly intimate and emotional contexts, necessarily leads to 'caring' or acts of moral or ethical responsibility or obligation: fundamentally important aspects of 'community' as it is commonly understood. This is not to say that these cannot exist on-line, but that it is important to question if they do and how they are manifested, and not to assume that connection, interactivity and the technical ability to 'share' necessarily evidence (or necessarily lead to) such behaviour. Indeed, as was demonstrated in the beginning of this paper, there is a great deal happening on-line suggesting that it does not.

Conclusion

Modern communications technology has the ability to remove many of the restrictions related to physical distance from our social life. Yet distance is not only a material or geographical matter; it is also a social and ethical one. It takes more than technology to overcome social and moral distances (Silverstone, 2003). As we have seen, in many respects, technology can even be used to create further social and ethical distances within a context of communicative proximity.

We live in a technological culture where the distinction between absence and presence is becoming increasingly complicated through the use of communications technologies. If we accept the premise that the way we behave towards each other and care for each other is in some manner affected by our presence or proximity towards each other, then a situation in which the distinction between absence and presence is undermined poses a potential ethical problem in that our spheres of influence and interaction with others or our social presences, are no longer contiguous with our horizons of care, feelings of ethical responsibility, or physical presence.

In this paper, I have suggested that this problem of presence can be articulated in two ways. First, on-line life exaggerates the metaphysical conceptualisation of presence upon which modern conceptions of being-in-the-world are based. This ultimately presents the world to us in instrumental terms, which, in terms of ethics, means that beings in the world are approached nihilistically: primarily as things to be used. Our use of technology merely intensifies this process, which ultimately Enframes social life itself, objectifying and instrumentalising human relations. Secondly, I argued that the material, bodily, face-to-face presence of others is the essence of ethical social encounter and the feeling of responsibility towards others. Mediated interaction moves us into a disembodied encounter where the other loses 'face' and substance, and therefore an ethical or moral compulsion.

In both cases, metaphysical presence encourages us to objectify others and this arguably means that our sense of moral and ethical responsibility to others is weakened in favour of a subject-centred, instrumental way of being. This creates a fundamental contradiction in contemporary culture, what I call a 'crisis of presence', in which we live in a world where we are increasingly connected and where our social horizons, interactions, influences and presences are less and less spatially limited, but our horizons of care or responsibility to others are still very much based on physical proximity.

This disjuncture is becoming increasingly evident in a number of social problems within digital culture as society now starts to struggle with the 'real world' consequences of on-line behaviour and a tendency to objectify mediated others. Examples such as on-line suicides, trolling, flaming and cyberbullying were used here as illustrative of such objectifying, instrumental tendencies in on-line life.[16]

A critical evaluation of on-line behaviour here was intended to highlight the fact that we need to come to terms with the potential moral and ethical consequences of our changing presence if we are going to continue to invest more of our social, economic and political lives in technologies that decouple physical and social presence. As we have seen, technology and the expanding spatial scale of life in contemporary capitalism have given the ability to move us away from the ethical realm of responsibility and care into a realm of abstraction. This inevitably moves responsibility for interpersonal behaviour from embodied humans to the abstract principles of state and the law (Bauman, 1993) or other abstract systems (Giddens, 1991). In the largely unregulated, somewhat liminal, and increasingly important, sphere of on-line social life, this has generally meant a push towards more formal regulation of interpersonal behaviour.

If we wish to avoid this trend, and perhaps even if we do not, the challenge for networked humanity is to recognise and resist the tendency towards abstraction and metaphysically inspired instrumentalism inherent in our cultural tendencies and use of technology. Here, two possibilities exist. On the one hand, we can, as Silverstone (2003) suggests, strive towards the creation of 'proper distance' in our ethical behaviour towards mediated others. To retool our horizons of care and responsibility in a way that retains the compulsion to care for the other, which emerges from a physical presence with the other. On the other hand, we can strive to change the nature of technologically mediated encounter away from mathematically reductionist interfaces to ones that better reveal humanity, expression and individuality (Lanier, 2010). Indeed, we can even attempt to increase a sense of embodied presence and proximity through the creation of more sensuous digital encounters—for example, through haptic technologies (Boothroyd, 2009). Such efforts could move some way towards re-establishing a link between physical and social presence and bring ethical encounter back into mediated communications.

Acknowledgements

The author would like to thank Johnny Ilan, Anne Alwis, two anonymous referees and the hillside behind Rutherford College at the University of Kent, for assistance in the completion of this paper.

Notes

1. It is important to state early on that the position put forward is not that information technologies cause unethical behaviour. Reasons for these behaviours can, and should be, seen as complex. I suggest that ethical behaviour results from certain ways of being present and that these are changed as we live more and more of our lives through the medium of communications technologies.
2. I am using the word 'presence' here in a similar manner to Gumbrecht (2004). He suggests that Heidegger's use of 'being' and his use of 'presence' are interchangeable. I agree with this and use them interchangeably in this essay.
3. In the 2006 Nikki Catsouras case, Miss Catsouras died in a high-speed collision with a California highway toll booth. Grisly accident scene photographs had been leaked into the Internet, which were then posted on fake Myspace pages in her name and even sent to parents and family members via e-mail by several sources.
4. "Hostile intensions characterised by words of profanity, obscenity, and insults that inflict harm to a person or and organisation" (Alonzo and Aiken, 2004: 205).
5. For example, in 2012, a German model, Claudia Boerner, subsequent to an appearance on a reality television programme ('The Perfect Dinner'), received a barrage of abuse via social media and e-mail to the point that she took her own life.
6. There is a big discrepancy among teens and adults in this study. For example, 20 per cent of teenagers, vs 5 per cent of adults, categorised their overall experience of behaviour on SNSs as 'mostly unkind'.
7. The term 'deindividuation' is used by psychologists to describe a situation where individuals, usually involved in groups and involving a certain degree of anonymity, lose their sense of individuality and thus personal responsibility for their actions, allowing them to engage in behaviour they would not otherwise.
8. Castellà et al. (2000) found that anonymity is not the determining factor in on-line abuse that is commonly assumed and suggest that "uninhibited behaviour is not then an inevitable consequence of anonymity, but instead depends on whether or not it forms part of the group norms" (Castellà et al., 2000, p. 144).
9. That is not to say that civility, kindness, affection and many other positive human interactions do not also exist, but to suggest that these more negative aspects are largely ignored within social science research, despite such behaviour being somewhat endemic.
10. The key exceptions here are Silverstone, 2007; Ploug, 2009; and Willson, 2012.
11. Dasein is usually translated as 'being-there', 'presence' or even 'unfolding existence'. Heidegger uses Dasein (along with being-in the-world) to describe the human condition of consciousness emerging from a living relationship with the world, while at the same time possessing an awareness of one's own existence and the finiteness of it.
12. These potentials are of course part of the optimism behind the potential of a revival of a 'public sphere' on on-line contexts as well.
13. The cybersexual encounter perhaps best sums up this relationship. On the one hand, this is very much an encounter rooted in the needs of the body and may well involve stimulation of the senses through the viewing of erotic materials; on the other, several studies suggest that such encounters are primarily experienced through imagination, idealisation and self-projection (Döring, 2000; Ross, 2005; Ben Ze'ev, 2004).
14. Statements such as "UNIX expresses too large a belief in discrete abstract symbols and not enough of a belief in temporal, continuous, nonabstract reality" (Lanier, 2010, p. 11) seem an almost

logical extension of Heidegger's critique of metaphysical presence in modern philosophy into the digital age.

15. The stranger here can be used as a substitution for the other, in the sense that the stranger refers to a figure of ambiguity, one who upsets cognitive, aesthetic and moral boundaries which separate 'us' from 'them' or 'we from 'they', thus strangers cannot fully be identified. The stranger is a continuous problem in modern (and particularly urban) life and produces a moral and ethical indecisiveness in our relationship to the other (Silverstone, 2006; see also Bauman, 1993).

16. However, more general concerns over privacy and crime in the digital age can also be seen as illustrative of this trend.

References

ADAMS, T. (2011) How the internet created an age of rage, *The Observer*, 24 July (http://www.guardian.co.uk/technology/2011/jul/24/internet-anonymity-trolling-tim-adams; accessed 25 June 2012).

AHO, K. (2009) *Heidegger's Neglect of the Body*. Albany, NY: State University of New York Press.

ALONZO, M. and AIKEN, M. (2004) Flaming in electronic communication, *Decision Support Systems*, 36, pp. 205–213.

ARISTOTLE (1984) *Rhetoric: Poetics*. New York: Modern Library.

BARNEY, D. (2004) *The Network Society*. Cambridge: Polity.

BARON, N. (2008) *Always On: Language in an Online and Mobile World*. Oxford: Oxford University Press.

BAUMAN, Z. (1993) *Postmodern Ethics*. Oxford: Blackwell.

BAYM, N. (2002) Interpersonal life online, in: L. LIEVROUW and S. LIVINGSTONE (Eds) *Handbook of New Media*, pp. 62–76. London: Sage.

BBC (2011) Facebook bullying suicide boy's parents in law change call, *News Online*, 12 July (http://www.bbc.co.uk/news/uk-england-birmingham-14121631; accessed 16 February 2012).

BEATBULLYING (2012) *Virtual violence II: progress and challenges in the fight against cyberbullying*. Commissioned by Nominet Trust in association with the National Association for Head Teachers, London (http://www2.beatbullying.org/pdfs/Virtual-Violence-II.pdf; accessed 10 February 2012).

BEN ZE'EV, A. (2004) *Love Online: Emotions on the Internet*. Cambridge: Cambridge University Press.

BERGO, B. (1999) *Levinas Between Ethics and Politics: For the Beauty That Adorns the Earth*. Dordrecht: Kluwer Academic.

BOELLSTORFF, T. (2008) *Coming of Age in Second Life*. Oxford: Princeton University Press.

BOLTANSKI, L. (1999) *Distant Suffering: Morality, Media, and Politics*. Cambridge: Cambridge University Press.

BOOTHROYD, D. (2009) Touch, time and technics: Levinas and the ethics of haptic communications, *Theory, Culture and Society*, 26(2/3), pp. 330–345.

CARR, N. (2011) *The Shallows: What the Internet is Doing to Our Brains*. New York: W. W. Norton.

CASTELLÀ, V., ABAD, A., ALONSO, P. and SILLA, J. (2000) The influence of familiarity among group members, group atmosphere and assertiveness or uninhibited behaviour through three different communication media, *Computers in Human Behavior*, 16, pp. 141–159.

CASTELLS, M. (1996) *The Rise of the Network Society*. Oxford: Blackwell.

CHOULIARAKI, L. (2008) The mediation of suffering and the vision of a cosmopolitan public, *Television and New Media*, 9(5), pp. 371–391.

DAKROURY, A. and BIRDSALL, W. (2008) *Blogs and the right to communicate: towards creating a space-less public sphere?* Paper presented at the *Institute of Electrical and Electronics Engineers International Symposium on Technology and Society*, Fredericton, New Brunswick (http://ieeexplore.ieee.org/stamp/stamp.jsp?arnumber=4559762andisnumber=4559749; accessed 26 January 2009).

DAVIS, C. (1996) *Levinas: An Introduction*. Cambridge: Polity Press.

DAY, G. (2006) *Community and Everyday Life*. New York: Routledge.

DÖRING, N. (2000) Feminist views of cybersex: victimization, liberation and empowerment, *Cyberpsychology & Behavior*, 3(5), pp. 863–884.

FERNBACK, J. (1999) There is a there there: notes toward a definition of cybercommunity, in: S. JONES (Ed.) *Doing Internet Research: Critical Issues and Methods for Examining the Net*, pp. 203–220. Thousand Oaks, CA: Sage.

FIGENSCHOU, T. (2011) Suffering up close: the strategic construction of mediated suffering on Al Jazeera English, *International Journal of Communication*, 5(3), pp. 233–253.

GERGEN, K. (2002) The challenge of absent presence, in: J. KATZ and M. AAKHUS (Eds) *Perpetual Contact: Mobile Communication, Private Talk, Public Performance*, pp. 227–241. Cambridge: Cambridge University Press.

GIDDENS, A. (1991) *Modernity and Self-identity: Self and Society in the Late Modern Age*. Cambridge: Polity.

GRINTER, D. and ELDRIDGE, M. (2001) Y do tngrs luv 2 txt msg? in: W. PRINZ, M. JARKE, Y. ROGERS, K. SCHMIDT and V. WULF (Eds) *Proceedings of the Seventh European Conference on Computer Supported Cooperative Work*, pp. 219–238. Dordrecht: Kluwer Academic Publishers.

GUMBRECHT, H. (2004) *Production of Presence*. Stanford, CA: Stanford University Press.

HAGUE, B. and LOADER, B. (eds.) (1999) *Digital Democracy: Discourse and Decision Making in the Information Age*. London: Routledge.

HAMMAN, R. (1996) Rhizome@Internet: using the Internet as an example of Deleuze and Guattari's 'Rhizome' (http://www.swinburne.infoxchange.net.au/media/halm316/gallery/david/pg11b. htm; accessed 15 June 2009).

HANSEN, M. (2006) *New Philosophy for New Media*. Cambridge, MA: MIT Press.

HARPER, R. (2010) *Texture: Human Expression in an Age of Communications Overload*. London: MIT Press.

HEIDEGGER, M. (1962) *Being and Time*. Oxford: Blackwell.

HEIDEGGER, M. (1977) *The Question Concerning Technology and Other Essays*. London: Harper and Rowe.

HODGE, J. (1995) *Heidegger and Ethics*. London: Routledge.

HURST, B. (2011) Suicide websites shut down call, *Birmingham Mail*, 11 January (http://blogs. birminghammail.net/technobabble/2012/01/suicide-website-shut-down-call.html; accessed 15 February 2012).

KEISLER, S.; SIEGEL, J.; and McGUIRE, T. (1984) *Social psychological aspects of computer-mediated communication*, American Psychologist, 39(10), pp. 1123–1134.

LANIER, J. (2010) *You Are Not a Gadget*. St Ives: Penguin.

LEVINAS, E. (1969) *Totality and Infinity: An Essay on Exteriority*. Pittsburgh, PA: Duquesne University Press.

LEVINAS, E. and NEMO, P. (1985) *Ethics and Infinity: Conversations with Philippe Nemo*. Pittsburgh, PA: Duquesne University Press.

LICOPPE, C. and SMOREDA, Z. (2005) Are social networks technologically embedded?, *Social Networks*, 27(4), pp. 317–335.

MANNING, R. and SHEFFLER, J. (1993) *Interpreting Otherwise Than Heidegger: Emmanuel Levinas's Ethics As First Philosophy*. Pittsburgh, PA: Duquesne University Press.

MILLER, D. and SLATER, D. (2000) *The Internet*. Oxford: Berg.

MOELLER, S. (1999) *Compassion Fatigue: How the Media Sell Disease, Famine, War, and Death*. New York: Routledge.

MOOR, P., HEUVELMAN, A. and VERLEUR, R. (2010) Flaming on YouTube, *Computers in Human Behavior*, 26, pp. 1536–1546.

MOROZOV, E. (2011) *The Net Delusion: How Not To Liberate the World*. London: Allen Lane.

ORGAD, S. (2005) *Storytelling Online: Talking Breast Cancer on the Internet*. New York: Peter Lang.

ORGAD, S. (2007) The internet as a moral space: the legacy of Roger Silverstone, *New Media and Society*, 9(1), pp. 33–41.

PAGANELLI, M. (2010) The moralizing role of distance in Adam Smith: *The Theory of Moral Sentiments as a possible praise of commerce*, History of Political Economy, 42(3), pp. 425–441.

PARISER, E. (2011) *The Filter Bubble: What the Internet is Hiding from You*. London: Viking.

PATTINSON, G. (2000) *The Later Heidegger*. London: Routledge.

PLOUG, T. (2009) *Ethics in Cyberspace: How Cyberspace May Influence Interpersonal Interaction*. London: Springer.

RAINIE, R., LENHART, A. and SMITH, A. (2012) *The Tone of Life on Social Networking Sites*. Pew Internet and American Life Project, Washington, DC (http://preinternet.org/Reports/2012/Social-networking-climate.aspx; accessed 12 April 2012).

RHEINGOLD, H. (2000) *The Virtual Community: Homesteading on the Electronic Frontier*, 2nd edn. Cambridge, MA: MIT Press.

ROJCEWICZ, R. (2006) *The Gods and Technology: A Reading of Heidegger*. Albany, NY: State University of New York Press.

ROSS, M. (2005) Typing, doing and being: sexuality and the Internet, *Journal of Sex Research*, 42(4), pp. 342–352.

SILVERSTONE, R. (2002) Complicity and collusion in the mediation of everyday life, *New Literary History*, 33, pp. 761–780.

SILVERTONE, R. (2003) Proper distance: towards an ethics for cyberspace, in: G. LIESTOL, A. MORRISON and R. TERJE (Eds) *Digital Media Revisited*, pp. 469–491. Cambridge, MA: MIT press.

SILVERSTONE, R. (2006) *Media and Morality: On the Rise of Mediapolis*. Cambridge, Polity.

SLACK, J. (2008) 'Suicide websites' to be banned following links to a string of young deaths… but new law won't affect foreign sites, *Daily Mail Online*, 17 September (http://www.dailymail.co.uk/news/ article-1056941/Suicide-websites-banned-following-links-string-young-deaths–new-law-wont-affect-foreign-sites.html; accessed 14 February 2012).

SMELIK, A. (2010) Mediating memories: the ethics of post-9/11 spectatorship, *Arcadia: International Journal for Literary Studies*, 45(2), pp. 307–325.

SMITH, A. (1959/1976) *The Theory of Moral Sentiments*. Oxford: Clarendon Press.

SMITH, D. (2000) *Moral Geographies: Ethics in a World of Difference*. Edinburgh: Edinburgh University Press.

SONTAG, S. (2003) *Regarding the Pain of Others*. London: Penguin.

STONE, A. R. (1995) *The War of Desire and Technology at the Close of the Mechanical Age*. Cambridge, MA: MIT Press.

TESTER, K. (2001) *Compassion, Morality, and the Media*. Buckingham: Open University Press.

TOKUNAGA, R. (2010) Following you home from school: a critical review and synthesis of research on cyberbullying victimization, *Computers in Human Behavior*, 26, pp. 277–287.

TURKLE, S. (1996) *Life on the Screen: Identity in the Age of the Internet*. London: Weidenfeld & Nicolson.

TURKLE, S. (2011) *Alone Together: Why We Expect More from Technology and Less from Each Other*. New York: Basic Books.

USA TODAY (2012) Cyberbullying suicides (http://mediagallery.usatoday.com/Cyberbullying+ suicides/G3221, accessed 15 February 2012).

WHITE, C. (1996) The time of being and the metaphysics of presence, *Man and World*, 29, pp. 147–166.

WILLSON, M. (2012) Being-together: thinking through technologically mediated sociality and community, *Communication and Critical/Cultural Studies*, 9(3), pp. 279–297.

WISE, J. (1997) *Exploring Technology and Social Space*. London: Sage.

Political Presence and the Politics of Noise

KIRSI PAULIINA KALLIO

Abstract. The paper is inspired by the recent turn taking place at the intersection of critical citizenship studies and political geography where the meanings of political agency are being contested and re-imagined. As one major theme, this discussion involves the identification of political agency in the practice of everyday life. To introduce a new analytical approach into this line of research, the paper discusses political presence with reference to Jacques Rancière's conceptualisation of politics. By linking his thought with present spatially grounded debates on citizenship and political agency, it considers how the politics of noise can be identified from young people's everyday encounters with their political communities.

Introduction

In her two recent articles, Lynn Staeheli (2010, 2011) takes up the concept of citizenship from a political geographical perspective. By introducing a vast array of research she points out the "continual rearticulations of the relationships and sites through which citizenship is constructed" (Staeheli, 2011, p. 393) and the "material and virtual spaces for public address in which groups struggle to expand, and in some cases reorder, democratic publics" (Staeheli, 2010, p. 67). Along similar lines, Luke Desforges *et al.* (2005) present theoretical and methodological inroads into the geographies of citizenship, arguing that the flow of ideas should not be solely extracted from citizenship studies into geographical sub-disciplinary research, but that geographers themselves also possess an array of analytical tools other than 'space' which they can offer to interdisciplinary discussion. Other examples of this trend where political geographical ideas are employed in challenging normative notions of citizenship and political agency are articles by Fernando Bosco (2010) and Sarah Elwood and Katharyne Mitchell (2012), discussing children's political agency and practice. These papers' explicit agenda is not to reformulate the concept of citizenship, but to provide new approaches to thinking about political agency by introducing children's political practices in their mundane intergenerational relations.

These examples demonstrate the on-going and vivid discussions which seek to bring together critical citizenship studies approaches, political geographical theorisation and pertinent discussions from a number of sub-disciplinary fields that have started to question the established notions of political agency and citizenship as status, membership and practice. Wishing to contribute to this debate, this paper introduces the concept of political presence for the study of the hidden and imperceptible forms of political agency. Drawing from Jacques Rancière's (1992, 1999, 2001) conception of politics, I suggest that the political aspects of mundane spatial practice can be made more comprehensible if identified as politics of noise. By blurring the line between voiced and voiceless modes of active citizenship, this approach disrupts the binary of political absence and presence.

One of Rancière's main arguments is that, if we wish to understand the political as it unfolds in the world, we should not be content to get acquainted with the politics of order but should search for the ruptures where this order is disturbed by the politics of disagreement. Taking this as a starting-point, I present some analytical ideas that help to notice political presence at the back and in the centre of such ruptures. Like Bosco (2010) and Elwood and Mitchell (2012), I do not aim to reconceptualise citizenship *per se* but, rather, consider the unfolding of political agency in (early) youth. Empirically, the paper engages with some Finnish youths whose practices of everyday life provide apt examples of mundane political agency that differs notably from the more conventional acts of citizenship.

The paper proceeds as follows. First, I provide an overall contextualisation for the article, introducing the dilemma of the discussed young people's political agency and the pertinent scholarly discussion. I then present the analytical frame and my reading of Rancièrian politics. To flesh these out, I bring in an empirical case where politics of noise can be traced with the provided analytical tools. In conclusion, I discuss how the developed approach may, among other things, help to overcome some ambiguities related to normativity in the study of citizenship and political agency.

The Dilemma of Young People's Political Agency

Young people's interest in politics, their concerns over societal issues and their readiness to participate in public matters are declining in many liberal democracies. This development has been found alarming in Europe, North America, Australasia and beyond (Gray and Caul, 2000; O'Toole, 2003; Forbrig, 2005; Nasrallah, 2009). At the same time as the Arab Spring exposed youth's potential to claim democratic rights and initiate political change, in many European countries young people do not seem to appreciate their given rights to take part in societal matters through official or even semi-official channels (Staeheli 2013). Surprisingly, this trend is particularly apparent in places that are well known for their functional democratic system and civil obedience, such as Finland.

According to the recent survey of the International Association for the Evaluation of Educational Achievement (IEA), Finnish young people's level of interest and readiness to participate in politics and civic involvement are exceptionally low (Schulz *et al.*, 2010). The annually conducted national Youth Barometer (Myllyniemi, 2010, p. 100) supports this finding, indicating that youth's interest in civil society and communal action has diminished notably in the past 10 years. Yet there is a certain contradiction embedded in this trend. At the same time as the IEA identifies low levels of political interest and participation, Finnish young people are found to be more knowledgeable in societal matters than their peer groups in other countries and their trust in political institutions is very high. This finding has been made in a number of international comparative assessments that repeatedly portray the educational results of Finnish schools as top level (for example, the OECD Programme for International Student Assessment, PISA).[1]

This dilemma, problematic in its own right, appears even more awkward when placed in the prevailing policy climate. Finnish child and youth policies are deeply rooted in the United Nations' Convention on the Rights of the Child (UNCRC) that provides children with universal rights to protection, provision and participation (Kallio and Häkli, 2011a).[2] Since the ratification of the UNCRC in 1991, children's right to be heard and participate in matters concerning them has been taken to the fore by researchers, policy-makers and child rights activists (Strandell, 2010). As a result, participation has become an unquestionable right of the child that is acknowledged in supranational policies (for example, the European Union White Paper on Youth 2001), national legislation (for example, the Finnish Youth Act 2006; the Finnish Child Welfare Act 2007[3]), municipal strategies (for example, the City of Tampere Child and Youth Policy Strategy and Child Welfare Plan 2009–2012[4]), as well as in numerous agenda-setting policy documents (for example, The Finnish Government Child and Youth Policy Programmes 2007–2011, 2012–2015[5]). With regard to citizenship, children and young people's active roles are hence much appreciated, noticed and provided for.

Together, these facts raise the question: why are the Finnish young people not interested in acting in and for their communities when they *trust* the prevailing political system, are *knowledgeable* and *aware* of the societal issues and problems of their worlds, and have *means* and *arenas* to participate and take action in matters important to them? If compared with their coevals on the other side of the Mediterranean Sea, they appear as apolitical, immature and apathetic citizens, and not as active political beings. How should we understand the development and unfolding of political agency in situations where people are given broad opportunities as citizens from early on, yet they seem to scorn everything that has to do with their communities and the society at large? The next section provides an entry point towards understanding this puzzle.

Unravelling Youthful Political Agency

One way to start unravelling this dilemma is to look into the interpretations and implementation of children and young people's rights. Since the establishment of the UNCRC, it has become evident that the fulfilment of these universal rights involves major difficulties. In particular, the reconciliation of children and young people's rights to protection/provision and their participatory rights has proved problematic (for example, Franklin, 2002; Kallio, 2012). The main reason is not disagreement on the *significance* of the latter—rather, there is a notable difference of opinion on its *meanings*. The drafting process of the Convention itself exposed a considerable discord on how the right to be heard should be understood, who is responsible for listening to children, where children are supposed to express themselves and on which grounds their views should be supported and furthered (Moosa-Mitha, 2005; OHCHR, 2007). Since then, both the core of and the limits to this right have been constantly shifting and blurred, depending on how, by whom, where and on which grounds they are construed.

Consequently, the problems related to children and young people's participation have received increasing attention within academia. Their active agencies and roles have been debated in the context of legal procedures (Ruddick, 2007; Archard and Skivenes, 2009), armed conflicts (Goodwin-Gill and Cohn, 1994; Brocklehurst, 2006), social work and child care (Vandenbroeck and Bouverne-de Bie, 2006; Forsberg and Strandell, 2007), school (Bragg, 2007; Thomas, 2009; Lazar, 2010), community development and planning (Percy-Smith, 2006; Murtagh and Murphy, 2011), cultural politics and work (Stephens, 1995; Shepher-Hughes and Sargent, 1998; Katz, 2004), civil activity and activism (Skelton and Valentine, 2003; Bosco, 2010) and beyond. This vivid discussion has brought to light the contextual nature of children and young people's social roles and agencies. The importance of noticing the differing geo-economic and socio-cultural environments where childhood and youth are led is ever more emphasised and the ambiguity embedded in the three-fold set of rights has become more explicit as these are implemented concurrently in various empirical contexts (Wyness *et al.*, 2004; Lund, 2007).

This discussion is largely organised around two intertwined yet distinguishable interpretive strands. On the one hand, participation is taken to mean agency that unfolds in children's everyday lives—engagement in the mundane activities of the home, the school, hobbies, peer groups, social media, local communities, etc. On the other hand, participation is understood as active involvement that takes place on public and (semi-)official arenas, such as court houses, parliamentary apparatuses, school boards, NGOs, youth organisations, demonstrations and on-line participation channels. Respectively, the promotion of participation has come to mean very different things, both in research and policy-making. Whereas some think that their positions should be strengthened primarily by supporting their mundane engagements, others accentuate the importance of involving children and young people in formal public action.

Depending on which orientation is emphasised, somewhat different kinds of political worlds are imagined as the context of children and young people's active agency. The former approach identifies the political community as experienced, enacted and defined in the everyday practices of childhood and youth. The latter, instead, locates participation more in the formal political community. Neither one of these interpretations is unwarranted—it has become evident that even young children and early youth can act as participants in political communities in both senses (for example, Bosco, 2010; Skelton, 2010). Yet the identification between these differently reasoned worlds is of utmost importance for making sense of youthful citizenships and political agencies.

The recognition of formal and informal political worlds as entwined but distinctive realities forms the node where the already-introduced dilemma can be disclosed. Civic education and participatory policies usually attempt to provide children and young people with information, tools and arenas for participation taking place in the formal political community, ranging from purely institutional (for example, school councils, child parliaments) to semi-formal (for example, demonstrations) and occasionally even activism-related activities (for example, social movements). Simultaneously, the surveys that seek to measure their interest and readiness to participate, and awareness of political matters, are motivated by and oriented towards thus the organised political world.

However, children and young people's opinions, orientations and interests are not grounded merely there but, at least as closely, in the political communities that unfold in their everyday lives. That is, the lived communities of the home, the school, the neighbourhood, hobbies, social media and the like. It is in these socially constructed worlds—spatially situated along the lines of transnational, local or otherwise relational citizenship rather than on territorially bounded municipal, national and cosmopolitan grounds (Staeheli 2011, p. 397; see also Koefoed and Simonsen, 2012)—that children and young people acquire unquestionable positions, roles, identities, subjectivities and interests through, by and for which to act and develop as political agents (Kallio and Häkli, 2011b). These worlds are rarely considered as focal when young people's political orientations and activities are surveyed.

Put together, civic education, institutional participatory practices and assessment processes are typically concerned with political realities that differ eminently from the ones where children and young people are spontaneously most active and have things at stake. By concentrating on formal political communities, they therefore do not succeed in identifying, touching upon or measuring youthful agents' devotedness and activities in their *lived* political worlds. This blindness to children and young people's political realities derives from the common conception where they are not thought to lead political lives in the first place, unless specifically involved. However, they do, as is being increasingly noticed in the topical research (for example, Lister, 2007; Thomas, 2009; Bosco, 2010; Skelton, 2010; Staeheli, 2010; Strandell, 2010; James, 2011; Bartos, 2012; Elwood and Mitchell, 2012; see also the forthcoming Special Issue of *Space and Polity*, 17(1)).

Youthful agents' political presence escapes our attention because the forms of action developed and employed by them, their articulations of the matters important to them, their tactics of politicisation and the contexts where their political agencies mobilise, are often distinct from the politics familiar to us, as adults and researchers. Therefore, the power relations of childhood institutions and peer cultural communities, the norms and moralities that the young people follow, resist and negotiate in their everyday lives, their practices of care and social responsibility, and the bonds that children and young people build and protect in their personal relationships, are noticeably *absent* when their politics are considered. Yet it is these very practices and relationships through which they make *present* their intersubjective political agencies.

Analytical Tools for Studying Political Presence

The analytical tools introduced here derive from our on-going theorisation of political agency at the University of Tampere Space and Political Agency Research Group (see for example, Kallio and Häkli, 2011a, 2011b). Briefly put, we approach political agency in relational terms as a particular way of relating to the world, extending beyond rationality, formal know-how and determined involvement. The premise of this interpretation is the understanding of 'the political' as constantly contested and remade in social practice, and subjectivity as the condition of possibility of human political agency. For empirical research, this entails that the politics of any action, dynamics and processes are defined and analysed context-specifically (see Elwood and Mitchell, 2012).

This paper sets out to further develop our model for distinguishing different modes and spaces of children's politics (Kallio and Häkli, 2011a; see also Bartos, 2012; Wood, 2012). The model expands the dimensions of 'the political' along two intersecting continua: explicitness and reflexivity. The former refers to the degree to which 'the political' is readily identified and defined (known–contested–unidentified politics), underlining the distinction between political and 'apolitical' agency as unclear and unsettled (horizontal axis). The latter conveys the actors' reflexivity of the politics of their action (vertical axis). Based on this field, Figure 1 depicts political presence in terms of political involvement and political engagement, covering a whole range of settings where people find themselves as members of political communities.

Horizontally, the field of political presence is set from the community point of view, stressing the contextuality of 'the political': what is 'known' as politics varies from place to place, including the temporal element. As indicated in Figure 1, political engagement is more often linked with the not-yet-politicised issues than political involvement where established, recognised and contested political matters are typically more at stake. The vertical dimension is explicitly actor-centred, portraying self-identification in political community (understood as inseparably connected with social recognition). This identification is not necessarily reflexive, openly articulated or leaning on a particular (political) imagination or vocabulary. It ranges from feelings of belonging to understanding of social positions to acknowledgement of partisanship to intentional membership, and anything in between. In general, political involvement is more explicitly perceived than political engagement but, depending on the context and the people, this may mean very different things.

The analytical field presented in Figure 1 brings together relational political geographical thought and Rancière's (1992, 1999, 2001) conceptualisation of politics by coupling political engagement with 'politics of noise' and framing political involvement as 'politics of voice'. Those familiar with Rancière's theorisation will realise that this is not the obvious choice, but involves a particular reading of his work. In his original thought, 'noise' does not belong to the political

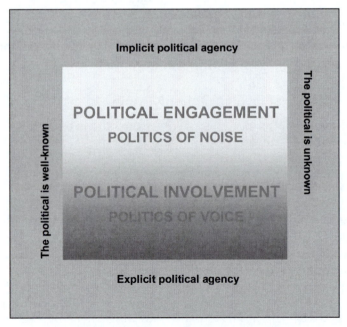

Figure 1. The field of political presence.

world (*la politique*) as such but becomes politics (*le politique*) only when it translates into 'voice'—i.e. succeeds in entering, being heard and interrupting the ordered political world of policy (*police*). This stems from the fact that unlike many political geographers (e.g. Skelton 2010), Rancière does not make the distinction between 'Politics' and 'politics'. Instead, he divides the world into the established order of things where politics implies a disruption through a reconfiguration of what he calls 'the system of partitioning' (Dikeç, 2005, p. 186; Swyngedouw, 2009). The potential of voice is, anyhow, always grounded in noise that is produced by the people beyond the policy order. Here 'people' refers to the subject of democracy that holds "the power of the *one more*, the power of *anyone*" (Rancière, 1992, p. 59; original emphasis) and not to calculable and measurable members of a certain community (i.e. population).

In Rancière's society the sum is always more than its parts combined. Therefore, the "unaccounted for"—the people acting from undefined starting-points—may confuse the right ordering of policy (Rancière, 1999, p. 11). Noise is produced by anyone who acts from without the order and, hence, can be returned to no-one in particular. As 'pure sound' this conception of noise/voice parallels Foucault's (2003, pp. 6–8) idea of "local knowledges" that are defined by their unlikeness to any qualified knowledge.[6] According to Foucault such disqualified knowledges can be desubjugated in a genealogical reading that is

> about the insurrection of knowledges … primarily, an insurrection against the centralizing power-effects that are bound up with the institutionalisation and workings of any scientific discourse organized in a society such as ours (Foucault, 2003, p. 9).

In Rancière's terms such a practice

> makes visible what had no business being seen, and makes heard a discourse where once there was only place for noise; it makes understood as discourse what was once only heard as noise (Rancière, 1999, p. 30).

In my attempt to bring Rancière's conceptualisation to the analysis of spatially grounded political presence, I concur with Davide Panagia (2009, see also Sloop and Gunn, 2010). Leaning on Michel de Certeau's (1984) key ideas on the politics of everyday life, Panagia notes that

> by extending our conceptions of what counts as sources for political disputes beyond the grammatical and hermeneutic limits of the semantic statement and the deliberative limits of the philosophical argument, we discover modes of political expression that don't simply rely on the need to communicate sense but nonetheless generate noise [creating] an 'espace lisible' of what de Certeau refers to as 'the art of nonsense'; 'the art of beginning or re-beginning to speak by saying' (Panagia, 2009: 72).

Along these lines, I associate politics of noise with people's everyday engagements with their political communities while politics of voice refers to more explicit involvement, directed towards or at least someway aware of the formal and 'known' world of politics (Figure 1).

I wish to stress that this analytical division is an attempt to clarify between different modes of political presence, not to separate diverse forms of politics categorically. As O'Toole (2003) and Skelton (2010) have aptly pointed out, young people's worlds that I will next turn to discussing do not neatly divide into two political realities. However, the division can be found useful in bringing to light those forms of political presence that first appear as political absence. As my aim is to develop analytical tools for studying the hidden and imperceptible forms of political agency, the rest of the paper concentrates on tracing engagement/noise from young people's mundane practice.

Young People's Political Presence at the Kiikeli Park

The Kiikeli Park case[7] does not present an uncommon tale but, rather, a story familiar from a number of urban studies projects where certain people's use of public space starts to appear problematic as that part of the city is zoned, built and inhabited, leading to an urban conflict. These events takes place in Oulu, Finland, in the early 2000s when the area was zoned and built. Prior to this, it was a stretch of unplanned downtown district that provided a place to 'hang out' for those who were not welcome in the city centre—namely, young people, the homeless and others who typically find little comfortable space in the urban commercial district. As Oulu was growing rapidly, the city decided to turn this wasteland into a city quarter that blurs the line between public and private urban space. The park is situated right in the centre of the city at the sea shore and it consists of two parts that are seamlessly connected with each other: a public recreation area and a smallish residential area. Next to these lies a boat harbour that is employed by private boaters but run by the city, and a marketplace together with an old market hall. It thus provides an inviting living environment particularly for affluent seniors.

The city planners, the building firms and the buyers of the apartments expected that once the area was physically transformed, the user groups would change as well. Problems emerged as it became apparent that this was not the case. When the park was completed, young people in particular returned to the park to 'hang out' during their summer holidays. Their activities consisted mostly of partying—i.e. getting drunk, playing loud music, driving around with mopeds and socialising in large groups at nights. Annoyed by this disturbance, the housing co-operatives began to file complaints to the city who were at first reluctant to deal with the case but, as the situation worsened, were forced to start 'cleaning' the area. For the first four years, the city tried to solve the disturbances with 'soft techniques' (enhancing the park facilities, waste collection and disposal, surveillance, routine policing, etc.). Since these did not have the desired effect, they attempted to close the park down by gating it. As this was barred by the Ministry of the Interior Police Department who declared it unconstitutional to privatise a public area, the park was only partially gated, together with the imposition of other policing measures which, finally, succeeded in displacing the young people.

Instead of looking into the struggle itself in more detail, I now turn to the political agency of the Kiikeli Park youth. Living in a Western liberal democracy with good opportunities to participate in formal politics but little interest to do so, they form an example *par excellence* of the young people discussed at beginning of this paper. As said, regardless of socioeconomic background or any other attribute, Finnish youth are well educated and rather knowledgeable and aware of societal issues. Almost all young people finish high school successfully and continue their studies at the upper secondary or vocational school, often with intentions to continue their studies in higher education. In the second place, the City of Oulu is very active regarding youthful civic involvement, having created their own model of municipal participation where children and young people are given plenty of specific chances to have their say on matters important to them.[8] They can participate in local youth councils whose members are selected at schools and youth centres; they can vote for and run as candidates in the youth delegate elections; they can make initiatives through an electronic system where they are assisted by the municipal youth workers; have their say in children and young people's open city meetings, and so on. This work is organised in collaboration with schools, parents and a number of NGOs, civic organisations and other (semi-)private actors (the church, hobbies, etc.).

Even if all of these measures were not in operation 10 years ago, the spirit was the same. This is to say that, had they wanted to fight against the gentrification process, NIMBY attitudes and their right to public space in general, there would have been many official, semi-official and informal quarters where the young people could have sought support. As the area was built partly for public use, it would have been possible to acquire a skating ramp or some other facility for the park—examples of such enterprises can be found in many equivalent planning processes in Finland (for example, Koskinen, 2010). Alternatively, they could have tried to involve their parents, the media or civic organisations to defend the park as a public and open space for the free use of all city dwellers. Or, they could have organised a peaceful demonstration in the form of a relaxed festival for professing their opinions about the appropriate use of the park. Yet the young people in this case did not appear to be interested in such action. Instead, they resisted the privatisation of the area by other means, by using it for their own purposes that were openly disapproved of by others.

As regards political presence, the Kiikeli Park young people's interest in political *involvement* was minimal, but they presented vast interest in political *engagement* in matters important to them. Instead of *voicing* their concerns, they were *noising* them in their practices of everyday life. Although this noise was not acknowledged as participation or active citizenship explicitly by anyone, it was certainly heard and recognised by a number of significant players (local residents, nearby businesses, municipal technical centre, communal social work, the police, local and national media, other townspeople, parents, etc.). Their presence also had many direct and indirect effects. First, for nearly 10 years, the Kiikeli Park area was lived in and dominated by these young people whereupon other people could make little use of it. Secondly, their particular presence forced the City of Oulu to take wide-ranging actions in the area, to the extent that they ended up challenging the constitutional law. Thirdly, the young people acquired experience and competence as political agents by participating in "'the politics of people' [that] wrongs policy", thus strengthening as citizen-subjects in their relational political worlds (Rancière, 1992, p. 59; see also Kallio and Häkli, 2011b; Staeheli, 2013). Fourthly, even though this participation was not reflected upon as explicitly political by anyone, it moulded the city as an urban system in a de Certeauian sense

> The act of walking is to the urban system what the speech act is to language or to statements uttered. At the most elementary level, it has a triple 'enunciative' function: it is a process of *appropriation* of the topographical system on the part of the pedestrian (just as the speaker appropriates and takes on the language); it is a spatial acting-out of the place

(just as the speech is an acoustic acting-out of language); and it implies *relations* among differentiated positions, that is, among pragmatic 'contracts' in the form of movements (just as verbal annunciation is an 'allocution', 'posits another opposite' the speaker and puts contracts between interlocutors into action). It thus seems possible to give a preliminary definition of walking as a space of enunciation (de Certeau, 1984, pp. 97–98; original emphases).

Returning to the dilemma of youthful political agency discussed at the beginning of the paper, the Kiikeli Park case provides an empirical site where the youngsters appear as politically apathetic or active, depending on whether their action is deciphered on formal or informal political grounds. From the civic education, participatory policies and democracy surveys points of view, these young people seem as politically absent, lacking both will and interest in any politics (of voice). Conversely, approached from their lived worlds, they can be recognised as closely engaged in politics (of noise). Considering that in Finland such fairly broadly recognised forms of political agency as squatting, *graffiti* and street occupation are often perceived in negative terms (for example, as illegal activism) and juxtaposed with more formal modes of citizenship (such as democratic practices at school), it is not surprising that the Kiikeli youth received relatively little public sympathy (see for example, Suutarinen and Törmäkangas, 2012; HS.fi, 2012).

Noise as Politics

Interpreting the noise generated by the Kiikeli Park young people as political presence takes us to the fringes of politics. If self-centred use of public space—be it individual or collective—is understood as political, what then does *not* fulfil the conditions of politics? This question is familiar to scholars working on everyday-life political issues, across disciplines (see for example, Brown, 2002; Dean, 2000, p. 8; Isin, 2005, p. 381). In current research, it is often met by considering politics separately from other aspects of social life. This interpretation, following Habermasian and Arendtian political theoretical traditions, has been employed by many scholars discussing young people's political agency, too. These include Tracey Skelton and Gill Valentine's (2003) and Sarah Elwood and Katharyne Mitchell's (2012) insightful approaches that provide tools for explaining the political aspects of the Kiikeli Park case. By stating that "Even if it does not take place through formal political structures or fora, young people can act as social and political agents and are competent to be involved", Skelton and Valentine (2003, p. 123) stress the importance of hearing noise as voice when applicable, and involving young people in their lived worlds. Elwood and Mitchell's approach, instead, appreciates young people's noise in itself as a form of political engagement

> Critical perceptions/judgments about inequality, subjectivity, and power relations enter the domain of the political when ... we can find evidence that children are recognizing and asserting themselves as particular subjects, in relation to others, to the structures in which they are situated, and to subject positions that may be imposed on them (Elwood and Mitchell, 2012, p. 4).

Setting off on different political theoretical grounds from these, the Rancièrian/de Certeauian reading of politics helps to reveal still some other fringes of politics.

Rancière's starting-point is that anything following the policy order or working along its lines cannot be political because, as an established social order, policy becomes "the 'naturally given' basis for government" (Dikeç 2005, p. 173). Instead of differentiating the political from the social, he dissociates it from *government*, reserving the concept of politics to the disruptions of the regime order

> Politics is not the enactment of the principle, the law, or the self of a community ... politics has no archê, it is anarchical (Rancière, 1992, p. 59; on *archê* [rule], see also Markell, 2006).

Moreover, as a whole, political life (*la politique*) can take place only in the intertwinement of policy (*police*) and politics (*le politique*), meaning that the policy order is maintained by the people only if the potential of politics exists to them. The potential of politics thus exists in the ruptures of the policy order. Yet Rancière does not suggest that this intertwinement inevitably leads to political *action*: it just denotes the *potential* for such.

De Certeau, instead, takes the next step by identifying that such 'free' agency is the prerequisite of human life. In the outline of his major work *The Practice of Everyday Life* (1984) he states

> The goal is not to make clearer how the violence of order is transmuted into a disciplinary technology, but rather to bring to light the clandestine forms taken by the dispersed, tactical, and makeshift creativity of groups or individuals already caught in the nets of 'discipline' (De Certeau, 1984, pp. xiv–xv).

These creative acts do not "obey the laws of the place, for they are not defined or identified by it" (p. 29). "Pushed to their ideal limits, these procedures and ruses of consumers compose the network of antidiscipline" (pp. xiv–xv). Continuing this thought, Tim Cresswell argues that

> These *tactics* refuse the neat divisions and classifications of the powerful and, in doing so, critique the spatialization of domination. Thus, the ordinary activities of everyday life ... become acts of heroic everyday resistance ... never producing 'proper places' but always using and manipulating places produced by others (Cresswell, 2006, p. 47; original emphasis).

As connoisseur of both Rancière and de Certeau, Panagia (2009) notices that bringing their ideas together is the key to discovering noise *as* politics. The de Certeauian reading of Rancière's theorisation suggests that mundane politics denotes disruptions of order that are practised by the groups and individuals who live under this rule, as part of their everyday lives. This political presence produces noise that forms the potential of voice but is also political in its own right. On these grounds, the young people of Kiikeli Park can be identified as political actors because they succeeded in confusing the right ordering of policy through creating noise—i.e. using public space in opposition to the common order, leading to disruption within it. The power of their politics lay in their very refusal to communicate with the other parties, their 'non-participation' (see O'Toole, 2003). They produced Foucauldian local knowledges that differed from all qualified knowledges and, thus, composed de Certeauian networks of antidiscipline that enabled them to act on their own grounds, beyond the dominant order that did not provide them with an equal position.

In this approach, the driving force of politics is the experienced imbalance of equality but its aim is not the production of new order but non-communicative disagreement. This is not to say that politics of noise could not turn into politics of voice in certain conditions, on some people's part, along the lines suggested by Skelton and Valentine (2003). Yet, expanding on Elwood and Mitchell (2012), this approach emphasises noticing noise as political in a specific meaning. To conclude, I discuss how this interpretive strand may help us to overcome some of the ambiguities related to normativity in the study of citizenship and political agency.

Recognising Politics

While discussing the politics of marginalised publics—such as children and young people, sexual and ethnic minorities, illegal immigrants and asylum-seekers—even critical research tends to highlight politics with which the scholars themselves can agree and, more often than not, wish to endorse. While taking such a normative approach, the research comes to evaluate the politics in question from one perspective or another. Problems arising from this research setting have been underlined in the critiques of recognition theories, for instance, by arguing that the ideals of open-ended social development and progress towards a better society are hard to reconcile (for example, Deranty and Renault, 2007; Markell, 2007; McNay, 2008). These critiques are often sympathetic with Rancière who is uncompromising in the matter. For him, the only lasting attribute of politics is equality, defined in a rather particular way

> Now for me the current dead end of political reflection and action is due to the identification of politics with the *self* of a community. ... the claim for identity on the part of so-called minorities against the hegemonic law of the ruling culture and identity. The big community and the smaller ones may charge one another with 'tribalism' or 'barbarianism', and both will be right in their charge and wrong in their claim. ... For the *primum movens* of policy is to purport to act as the self of the community, to turn the techniques of governing into natural laws of the social order. But if *politics* is something different from *policy*, it cannot draw on such an identification (Rancière, 1992, p. 59; original emphases).

Taking this reading of equality as its premise, the politics of noise approach negates the presumption that political action is always productive, beautiful, sensible, pleasant or desirable, even to those practising it. Rancière's principle of equality expects that we recognise also the politics that are not in our own interests and do not serve the common good—not in the meaning of acceptance but identification. Even the political normativity proposed by Deranty and Renault (2007, p. 102) that involves the "rejection of the order of things and the project of a fairer society" is incompatible with this thought, as it provides politics with a mission that it cannot have. Simply put, Rancière's (1999) politics is dis-agreement with order, whatever it may be, without the endeavour to generate new order.

The extent to which this recognition is practised or achieved in daily life is yet another question—a practical one, I would say. I am, for instance, not particularly happy when I see drunken youngsters in the neighbourhood park or when I find the traces of their parties 'in my backyard'. Yet if it occurs to me that their hanging around succeeds in piercing a rupture in the present order that seeks categorically to govern them—or to keep a rupture open for others to seize upon—should I dispute the politics of their presence merely because it is unpleasant to me and does not seem to involve a constructive element? Depending on the situation, I could answer 'yes' or 'no' but, if I stay true to Rancière, I must ask myself are not such events *par excellence* disagreements that prevent the order from becoming overpowering and, simultaneously, reveal its limitations and liminalities? Moreover, when it comes to children and young people who are in an intensive process of political becoming, should I not also appreciate their 'noise' as political because it forms the basis for all the 'voice' they can ever have? Where would the society end up if its children ceased to make noise?

These ambiguities, related to the normative aspects of political agency, led me to choose the Kiikeli Park case as the illustration in this paper. Politics of noise surely appear in different modes as well, many of which are much easier to acknowledge as political because of their apparent righteousness. In our on-going ethnographic study, we have encountered many ways in which children as young as 11 years of age engage in politics of noise, succeeding in disrupting the prevailing order. These include for instance individual and collective practices of care (such as peacefully counteracting peer cultural power relations involving inequalities), determined use of public space (such as walking the dog through park areas that are planned to be turned into a golf course extension) and non-commercial use of commercial space (such as using the shopping mall as a site for private fashion shows). Many would find it easier to agree with the politics of these acts as opposed to the Kiikeli Park young people's performance. Yet are they more valuable or real, or political, because they disclose desirable developments and activities? This is one of the essential questions that the Rancièrian conception of politics forces us to encounter.

If we take the question of general equality as seriously as Rancière does, we are compelled to ask how to contest categorisations by not replacing them with other categorisations and how to recognise political aspects in the forms of presence that are not relevant, advantageous or agreeable to our own politics. These questions are left untouched by Rancière and most of his followers who rarely seize upon the concrete problems of our lived worlds, leaving plenty of space for empirically grounded work at the political absence/presence interface. Returning to Staeheli's (2011) argument over contested and open-ended citizenship, is it not the noise of everyday life that continually rearticulates the relationships and sites through which political agency is constructed? If walking is the space of enunciation, as de Certeau (1984) suggests, what other spaces of re-articulation can be found through the ruptures created by people in their mundane presences?

Notes

1. See: http://www.pisa.oecd.org.
2. The UN defines the child as "every human being below the age of eighteen years unless under the law applicable to the child, majority is attained earlier" (http://www2.ohchr.org/english/law/crc. htm). In Finland, like in most liberal democracies, this right thus concerns all minors and, in part, also young adults up to their late 20s (see for example, the European Union White Paper on Youth 2001, http://eur-lex.europa.eu/LexUriServ/site/en/com/2001/com2001_0681en01.pdf; and the Finnish Youth Act 2006, http://www.finlex.fi/en/laki/kaannokset/1995/en19950235.pdf).
3. See: http://www.finlex.fi/en/laki/kaannokset/2007/en20070417.pdf.
4. See: http://www.tampere.fi/tiedostot/5pocaeMkx/lapsi_ja_nuorisopoliittinenohjelma.pdf.

5. See: http://www.okm.fi/export/sites/default/OPM/Julkaisut/2008/liitteet/opm21.pdf?lang=fi; http://http://www.minedu.fi/export/sites/default/OPM/Julkaisut/2012/liitteet/OKM8.pdf?lang=en.

6. To those more familiar with Foucault's thinking, this point of resemblance may help to see how Rancière's work interlinks with the relational political geographical perspectives where the P/political divide is taken as an analytical starting-point (see also Kallio, 2012). Yet, while making this parallel, it should be noted that Rancière's political philosophy can also be read as a partial critique to Foucault's thought, especially concerning his writings on governmentality. In a Rancièrian reading, the 'conduct of conduct' that is the imperative of governmental rationality may succeed only if the subjects are able to identify the potential of ruptures within the given regime. Foucault does not acknowledge such dependency between policy (*police*) and politics (*le politique*) that, to Rancière, forms the basic condition of political life (*la politique*).

7. The case is introduced here only very briefly because it is intended as a mere illustration, seeking to illuminate how politics of noise can be identified from mundane presence. For a more detailed account on the case and the research methodology, see Kallio and Häkli, 2011c.

8. See: http://www.ouka.fi/english/youth/youthcouncil.htm.

References

ARCHARD, D. and SKIVENES, M. (2009) Balancing a child's best interests and a child's views, *International Journal of Children's Rights*, 17(1), pp. 1–21.

BARTOS, A. (2012) Children caring for their worlds, *Political Geography*, 31(3), pp. 131–194.

BOSCO, F. (2010) Play, work or activism? Broadening the connections between political and children's geographies, *Children's Geographies*, 8(4), pp. 381–390.

BRAGG, S. (2007) 'Student voice' and governmentality: the production of enterprising subjects?, *Discourse: Studies in the Cultural Politics of Education*, 28(3), pp. 343–358.

BROCKLEHURST, H. (2006) *Who's Afraid of Children? Children, Conflict and International Relations*. Aldershot: Ashgate.

BROWN, W. (2002) At the edge, *Political Theory*, 30(4), pp. 556–576.

CERTEAU, M. DE (1984) *The Practice of Everyday Life*. Los Angeles, CA: University of California Press.

CRESSWELL, T. (2006) *On the Move: Mobility in the Modern Western World*. New York: Routledge.

DEAN, J. (2000) Introduction: the interface of political theory and cultural studies, in: J. DEAN (Ed.) *Cultural Studies and Political Theory*, pp. 1–19. Ithaca, NY: Cornell University Press.

DERANTY, J.-P. and RENAULT, E. (2007) Politicizing Honneth's ethics of recognition, *Thesis Eleven*, 88(1), pp. 92–111.

DESFORGES, L., JONES, R. and WOODS, M. (2005) New geographies of citizenship, *Citizenship Studies*, 9(5), pp. 439–451.

DIKEÇS, M. (2005) Space, politics and the political, *Environment and Planning D*, 23(2), pp. 171–188.

ELWOOD, S. and MITCHELL, K. (2012) Mapping children's politics: spatial stories, dialogic relations and political formation, *Geografiska Annaler: Series B*, 94(1), pp. 1–15.

FORBRIG, J. (Ed.). (2005) *Revisiting Youth Political Participation: Challenges for Research and Democratic Practice in Europe*. Strasbourg: Council of Europe.

FORSBERG, H. and STRANDELL, H. (2007) After-school hours and the meaning of home: re-defining Finnish childhood space, *Children's Geographies*, 5(1/2), pp. 393–408.

FOUCAULT, M. (2003) *Society Must Be Defended: Lectures at the College de France, 1975–1976*, transl. by D. Macey. New York: Picador.

FRANKLIN, B. (Ed.). (2002) *The New Handbook of Children's Rights: Comparative Policy and Practice*. London: Routledge.

GOODWIN-GILL, G. and COHN, I. (1994) *Child Soldiers: The Role of Children in Armed Conflicts*. Oxford: Clarendon Press.

GRAY, M. and CAUL, M. (2000) Declining voter turnout in advanced industrial democracies, *Comparative Political Studies*, 33(9), pp. 1091–1122.

HS.fi (2012) Tutkimus: Suomen nuoret ovat radikalisoituneet [Study: the Finnish youth have radicalised], *Helsingin Sanomat online*, 8 February.

ISIN, E. (2005) Engaging, being, political, *Political Geography*, 24(3), pp. 373–387.

JAMES, A. (2011) To be (come) or not to be (come): understanding children's citizenship, *The Annals of the American Academy of Political and Social Science*, 633(1), pp. 167–179.

KALLIO, K. P. (2012) Desubjugating childhoods by listening to the child's voice and childhoods at play, *ACME: An International E-Journal for Critical Geographies*, 11(1), pp. 81–109.

KALLIO, K. P. and HÄKLI, J. (2011a) Tracing children's politics, *Political Geography*, 30(2), pp. 99–109.

KALLIO, K. P. and HÄKLI, J. (2011b) Are there politics in childhood?, *Space & Polity*, 15(1), pp. 21–34.

KALLIO, K. P. and HÄKLI, J. (2011c) Young people's voiceless politics in the struggle over urban space, *GeoJournal*, 76(1), pp. 63–75.

KATZ, C. (2004) *Growing up Global: Economic Restructuring and Children's Everyday Lives*. Minneapolis, MN: University of Minnesota Press.

KOEFOED, L. and SIMONSEN, K. (2012) (Re)scaling identities: embodied Others and alternative spaces of identification, *Ethnicities*, DOI: 10.1177/1468796811434487.

KOSKINEN, S. (2010) *Lapset ja nuoret ympäristökansalaisina: ympäristökasvatuksen näkökulma osallistumiseen* [Children and young people as environmental citizens: environmental education approach to participation]. Helsinki: NTV/NTS.

LAZAR, S. (2010) Schooling and critical citizenship: pedagogies of political agency in El Alto, Bolivia, *Anthropology and Education Quarterly*, 41(2), pp. 181–205.

LISTER, R. (2007) Why citizenship: where, when and how children?, *Theoretical Inquiries in Law*, 8(2), pp. 693–718.

LUND, R. (2007) At the interface of development studies and child research: rethinking the participating child, *Children's Geographies*, 5(1/2), pp. 131–148.

MARKELL, P. (2006) The rule of the people: arendt, archê, and democracy, *The American Political Science Review*, 100(1), pp. 1–14.

MARKELL, P. (2007) The potential and the actual: Mead, Honneth, and the 'I', in: B. VAN DEN BRINK and D. OWEN (Eds) *Recognition and Power: Axel Honneth and the Tradition of Critical Social Theory*, pp. 100–132. New York: Cambridge University Press.

MCNAY, L. (2008) *Against Recognition*. Cambridge: Polity Press.

MOOSA-MITHA, M. (2005) A difference-centred alternative to theorization of children's citizenship rights, *Citizenship Studies*, 9(4), pp. 369–388.

MURTAGH, B. and MURPHY, A. (2011) Environmental affordances and children in post-conflict Belfast, *Space & Polity*, 15(1), pp. 65–79.

MYLLYNIEMI, S. (Ed.). (2010) *Puolustuskannalla: Nuorisobarometri 2010* [Youth Barometer 2010]. Helsinki: OKM, NTV and NUORA.

NASRALLAH, J. (2009) Voter turnout in Canada and Denmark, *Canadian Parliamentary Review*, Summer, pp. 33–37.

OHCHR (OFFICE OF THE HIGH COMMISSIONER FOR HUMAN RIGHTS) (2007) *Legislative History of the Convention on the Rights of the Child, Vol. 1*. New York: United Nations.

O'TOOLE, T. (2003) Engaging with young people's conceptions of the political, *Children's Geographies*, 1(1), pp. 71–90.

PANAGIA, D. (2009) *The Political Life of Sensation*. Durham, NC: Duke University Press.

PERCY-SMITH, B. (2006) From consultation to social learning in community participation with young people, *Children, Youth and Environments*, 16(2), pp. 153–179.

RANCIÈRE, J. (1992) Politics, identification, and subjectivization, *The Identity in Question*, 61, pp. 58–64.

RANCIÈRE, J. (1999) *Disagreement: Politics and Philosophy*. Minneapolis, MN: University of Minnesota Press.

RANCIÈRE, J. (2001) Ten theses on politics, transl. by R. Bowlby and D. Panagia, *Theory and Event*, 5(3), pp. 17–34.

RUDDICK, S. (2007) At the horizons of the subject: neo-liberalism, neo-conservatism and the rights of the child. Part one: from 'knowing' foetus to 'confused' child, *Gender, Place and Culture*, 14(5), pp. 513–527.

SCHULZ, W., AINLEY, J., FRAILLON, J., KERR, D. and LOSITO, B. (2010) *Initial findings from the IEA international civic and citizenship education study*. Amsterdam: International Association for the Evaluation of Educational Achievement.

SHEPHER-HUGHES, N. and SARGENT, C. (Eds). (1998) *Small Wars: The Cultural Politics of Childhood*. Los Angeles, CA: The University of California Press.

SKELTON, T. (2010) Taking young people as political actors seriously: opening the borders of political geography, *Area*, 42(2), pp. 145–151.

SKELTON, T. and VALENTINE, G. (2003) Political participation, political action and political identities: young d/deaf people's perspectives, *Space & Polity*, 7(2), pp. 117–134.

SLOOP, J. and GUNN, J. (2010) Status control: an admonition concerning the publicized privacy of social networking, *The Communication Review*, 13(4), pp. 289–308.

STAEHELI, L. (2010) Political geography: democracy and the disorderly public, *Progress in Human Geography*, 34(1), pp. 67–78.

STAEHELI, L. (2011) Political geography: where's citizenship?, *Progress in Human Geography*, 35(3), pp. 393–400.

STAEHELI, L. (forthcoming) Youth and citizenship: struggles on and off the street, *Space & Polity*, 17(1).

STEPHENS, S. (Ed.). (1995) *Children and the Politics of Culture*. Princeton, NJ: Princeton University Press.

STRANDELL, H. (2010) From structure–action to politics of childhood: sociological childhood research in Finland, *Current Sociology*, 58(2), pp. 165–185.

SUUTARINEN, S. and TÖRMÄKANGAS, K. (2012) Nuorten laittomaan aktivismiin valmiuden yhteys maahanmuuttajakriittisyyteen ja osallisuuskokemuksiin koulussa [Connection between young people's readiness to illegal activism, critical attitudes toward immigration and experiences of participation at school], *Nuorisotutkimus*, 30(1), pp. 70–89.

Swyngedouw, E. (2009) The antinomies of the postpolitical city: in search of a democratic politics of environmental production, *International Journal of Urban and Regional Research*, 33(3), pp. 601–620.

Thomas, M. (2009) The identity politics of school life: territoriality and the racial subjectivity of teen girls in LA, *Children's Geographies*, 7(1), pp. 7–19.

Vandenbroeck, M. and Bouverne-De Bie, M. (2006) Children's agency and educational norms: a tensed negotiation, *Childhood*, 13(1), pp. 127–143.

Wood, B. (2012) Crafted within liminal spaces: young people's everyday politics. *Political Geography*, 31(6), pp. 337–346.

Wyness, M., Harrison, L. and Buchanan, I. (2004) Childhood, politics and ambiguity: towards an agenda for children's political inclusion, *Sociology*, 38(1), pp. 81–99.

Knowing (or Not) about Katyń: The Silencing and Surfacing of Public Memory

DANIELLE DROZDZEWSKI

Abstract. For Poles, the Katyń Forest, in Russia, is a place immediately associated with national suffering. Katyń is one of three sites where approximately 20 000 Poles were executed during World War II, by the Soviet secret service. To shore up wartime political dependencies, knowledge of Katyń was silenced by the dominant hegemony. The public absence of Katyń narratives compelled their safeguarding and presence (where possible) in private spheres of the home. In 2010, the death of 96 people at Katyń—en route to commemorate the massacre—etched a new scar on an existing wound. The shifting of Katyń narratives between public absence and private presence exemplifies the importance of power in silencing public memory narratives.

Introduction

In Poland, and within Polish cultural memory, Katyń is a word immediately associated with mourning, loss of life and a politically and historically situated tenuous relationship with their Russian neighbours. Katyń refers to one of three main locations where approximately 20 000 Poles were executed in 1940 by the Soviet secret service (the People's Ministry of Internal Affairs, or NKVD). These executions occurred during the early stages of World War Two (WWII), when the Molotov–Ribbentrop Pact still allied Nazi Germany and Soviet Russia. From the executions until the fall of communism in eastern Europe, knowledge of the Katyń massacre, and most importantly the identity of its perpetrators, was veiled in secrecy. The public absence of the narrative was enforced to shore up existing political relationships and dependencies. Katyń was, and still is, a politically sensitive issue. These political underpinnings are not just historical. On the 70th anniversary of the massacre, a flight carrying the President and numerous high-ranking officials and intelligentsia crashed en route to a memorial service at Katyń, killing all 96 people on board. This time, news of the Katyń crash was publicly available within minutes. In 2010, 70 years after the original massacre, the presence of the Katyń narrative on the international stage meant that international audiences were learning not only about the contemporary plane crash, but also about the WWII massacre.

This paper will not focus on the minutiae of the investigations into the 1940 Katyń massacre.[1] Rather, it will chart how a politics of memory of Katyń has influenced the public availability of the Katyń narrative and trace how enforcing a discourse of absence led to the narrative's presence in private spheres. This paper has four key aims. First, it chronicles the Katyń story by contextualising it specifically within a politics of memory framework. Secondly, it draws on primary source data—interviews with Polish Australians—to exemplify the affect of a public silencing of Katyń on the everyday knowledges of Katyń. Thirdly, it examines the changing contexts of material commemoration of Katyń; using a landscape analysis it explains how the changing visibility and portrayals of the narrative in public spheres have been heavily linked to representations of Polish identity. Lastly, and unlike previous literature on Katyń, this paper extends the Katyń narrative to encompass the recent tragedy in 2010. This paper will weave these four elements in a chorological account of how the memory narratives have been both silenced and have (re)surfaced under the direction and influence of powerful hegemons. Moreover, this paper demonstrates how the absence and presence of Katyń memory narratives within different spaces depended on how power was exercised and controlled by dominant hegemonies. When and where the memory narratives were unable to surface publicly, due to the tight state-based control of public memory, the narratives remained, but were hidden within private spaces of the home and by families who knew about them. These private spaces were largely outside the state's control and policing of public spaces. Over a 50-year public silence, the Katyń narrative's continuance hinged on its concealment in private spaces and within families who knew about the WWII massacre.

This paper draws from a wider research project that utilised a mixed methods approach to understanding the linkages between cultural memory transmission and identity maintenance in Poland, and within Polish diaspora. Qualitative data sources including, semi-structured in-depth interviews, landscape observation and secondary and archival data sources, were scaffolded to (de)construct how memory narratives were (re)produced and transmitted to maintain Polish identities both in public spaces in Poland and within private spheres among Polish diaspora in Australia. Here, I examine the (re)production and transmission of one research theme—the Katyń massacre—and focus on how memory narratives about Katyń have been sourced, or not, and (re)produced despite a tightly controlled milieu of public surveillance. This paper utilises data from interviews held with a group of post-Socialist Polish migrants to Australia, who had experienced suppression of historical narratives and cultural memories first hand in Poland and had migrated to Australia in the 1980s. The interviews focused on how Polish cultural memories have been transmitted through generations of Polish families to maintain Polish identities. The interview data were teamed with critical readings of the memory landscape (see Duncan, 1990) and historical sources to enable a (de)construction of the absence and presence of Katyń memory narratives.

Part of this post-structuralist analysis of Katyń memories has been acknowledging my position as researcher and the way my situated knowledge in turn creates new (and contingent) interpretations of the Katyń story. While none of my own relatives died at Katyń, I have interviewed several post-WWII and post-Socialist migrants whose family members were murdered there. My Polish heritage means that the Katyń memory is part of my grandparents' history (and mine), yet I write this paper as partial outsider, as a non-Pole. The subsequent analyses are my interpretations of these articulations of memory, which are unavoidably linked to my positionality and the connection I feel to Polish cultural memories and histories in these places.

Positioning a Discourse of Absence and Power

A politics of memory concerns the control of memory information, its dissemination and its availability as part of public discourse. Mitchell has argued that

> Memory is bound up with power, and both memory and its corollary, forgetting, are hegemonically produced and maintained, never seamlessly or completely, but formidably and powerfully nonetheless (Mitchell, 2003, p. 443).

At each stage of the story of Katyń, a politics of memory has played an influential role in the control and public release of (mis)information about the massacre. Each stakeholder group, whether the Polish WWII government-in-exile in London, the Soviet Politburo, the Allies, or post-WWII Polish governments, have taken part in what Nowak (2011, p.1) has called a "clash of collective memories and identities". This conflict has arisen because the imposed silencing of Katyń has been crucial to the legitimacy and authority of several regimes and governments, both during and after WWII, and again after the dissolution of the Soviet Union. Moreover, for the Poles, *their* memory of Katyń is an integral, but long-inaccessible fragment of collective cultural memory that gives credence to a narrative of struggle and suffering for autonomy (Drozdzewski 2008).

Geographers, historians, sociologists and political scientists have explored the binding of memory and power (Edkins, 2003; Forrest and Johnson, 2011; Hayden, 1995; Hoelscher and Alderman, 2004; Mitchell, 2003; Stangl, 2008). Most commonly, analyses of memory and power have focused on the role of totalitarian and post-totalitarian states in (re)producing public memory discourses, and of the material outcomes of memory in everyday public spaces (Argenbright, 1999; Foote *et al.*, 2000; Forrest and Johnson, 2002; Light *et al.*, 2002; Nagel, 2002). These studies have uncovered how memory narratives and discourses of national identity have been (re)defined. Such (re)definition commonly involves new regimes creating alternative discourses of identity that accord with their political agenda (Hershkovitz, 1993). These newly (re)constructed national memories are given voice in monuments and memorials, among other outlets, creating sites for collective commemoration and the rallying of new shared memories. Such memorials are manifold in Eastern Europe, as has been the propensity for change in the memory landscape as regimes change and refocus their collective memories (Forrest and Johnson, 2002). Yet the Katyń story is complex because, while (re)productions of Katyń memories have been heavily influenced by the Soviet Union and the post-WWII Soviet-led Polish government, other democratic governments have also played a role in determining how and if the narrative is remembered.

The elements of a nation's past that are represented publicly are always 'chosen'. As Mitchell (2003, p. 443) has contended "there is a deep politics to memory". The power of choice of memory selection is utilised not only by authoritarian regimes, but also by democratic governments. 'Power' refers not only to selection of specific memories by overt oppression, but also in a Gramscian sense whereby a politics of memory creates naturalness and normality around a chosen memory narrative. That normality is rationalised and achieved by obtaining mainstream consensus around carefully selected events representing 'their' collective image of the national past. Dominant groups (democratic or otherwise) create *norms* of memory, quite deliberately and otherwise, which become ubiquitous and unquestioned narratives, commemorations and representations of a nation's past (Hay *et al.*, 2004; Johnson, 1995).

In the Katyń case, a number of powerful governments selectively remembered and forgot the massacre to suit their own needs. The most striking outcome of this selectivity was silence. The 50-year silence of the Katyń narrative in Soviet-controlled Eastern Europe, deprived the Polish nation of the opportunity to grieve and commemorate the deaths of a significant portion of its wartime army, or to receive international recognition of the collective deep scepticism of Soviet innocence. Kapuściński (1986, p. 189) has argued that silence is "the same sort of political instrument as the clatter of weapons or a speech at a rally", while Esbenshade (1995, p. 87) has contended that 'to forget'—in effect, to silence—is not simply the opposite of 'to remember'. Rather, forgetting is a process of selectively 'remembering otherwise'. The articulation of this process in public spheres is an "architecture of organised forgetting" (Sargin, 2004, p. 660), where power simultaneously influences both remembering and forgetting. As Kapuściński (1986, p. 186) also says, "silence is necessary to tyrants and occupiers, who take actions to have their actions accompanied by quiet". The creation and maintenance of a discourse of absence of the narrative were in themselves a form of oppression (Dunn, 2004).

The manipulations and the public silencing of Katyń memories, to be discussed in further detail, had differing effects on the everyday knowledge of the event among Poles in Poland, and Poles in diaspora. In Poland, knowing about Katyń was not as simple as reading a textbook on Polish history or looking for it on a map—records of this type were expunged to maintain the strictly controlled silence. Some Poles knew about Katyń from within very trusted circles, primarily within the home and the family. Two clearly demarcated spaces of knowledge existed—public and private. The private spheres discussed in this paper are the homes and families of Polish migrants interviewed for this research. The public spheres comprise the material aspects of the landscape, such as parks, streets, meeting places (Staeheli and Mitchell, 2007), but also public discourse including the open discussion of Polish cultural memories. The processes of remembering and forgetting Katyń have occurred concurrently and disparately in the public and private spheres, both being influenced by powerful hegemon(s) deciding what information to broadcast about Katyń. The reasons and timing of these decisions are elaborated in the following discussion.

Chronicling the Politics of Katyń

Poland's geographical position, between two powerful former empires—Germany and Russia—has been the root of many misfortunes. During World War II, Poland stood on each regime's pathway to victory. Westward expansion by the Soviets resulted in the annexing of the Eastern territories lost in the Polish–Soviet War (1920)—in present-day Ukraine and Belarus—as well as beginning a process of cultural cleansing (Allbrook and Cattalini, 1995). For the National Socialists, eastward domination would mean a place to resettle thousands of displaced persons (Burleigh, 1988).

The secret signing of the Molotov–Ribbentrop Pact between Soviet Russia and Nazi Germany saw the Soviets enter Polish territory on 17 September 1939. Met with little resistance on the Eastern Front—as Poland was largely unaware that it was under attack from Russia as well as Nazi Germany—many Polish officers, reservists, policeman, doctors, lawyers, scouts, non-commissioned officers were captured and, along with ordinary citizens, deported to various parts of the Soviet Union. Approximately 320 000 Poles were deported to places such as Siberia and to the gulags (IPN, 2008).

The fate of approximately 20 000 Poles, mostly military officers, but also police and intelligentsia, followed a different pathway. From October 1939, almost 15 000 of these prisoners were interned by the NKVD in three 'special' camps: Ostaszków, Kozielsk and Starobielsk (Figure 1). These camps were "set aside for officers, policemen, senior state and military officials, persons responsible for state security and military settlers" (IPN, 2004). An additional 7000 prisoners were interned in seven other smaller camps scattered through the Western Ukraine and Western Belarus. The prisoners were subjected to "mass propaganda intended to change their negative attitudes towards communism and the USSR [United Soviet Socialist Republics]" (IPN, 2004).

On 5 March 1940, Stalin approved and signed the proposal from Lavrentii Beria—chief of the NKVD—to execute the prisoners in the special camps. This

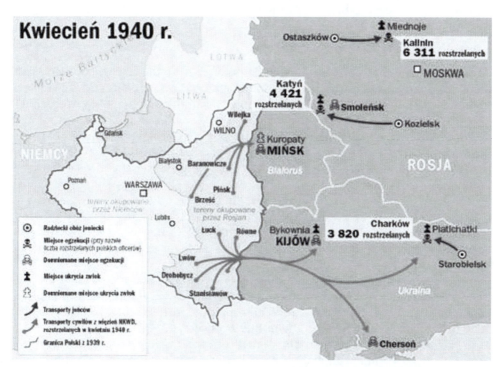

Figure 1. Locations of Katyń executions. *Source*: http://en.poland.gov.pl/ Commemoration,of,the,Katyn,Crime,Events,7072x329.html [Permission sought from the Polish Ministry of Foreign Affairs].

execution order was also signed by other key members of the Politburo, including: Kilment Voroshilov, Vyacheslav Molotov, Anastas Mikolyan, Mikhail Kalinin and Lazar Kaganovich. The execution orders described the prisoners as "avowed enemies of Soviet authority, filled with hatred of the Soviet system" (IPN, 2004). The executions were intended to rob the Polish nation of a sizeable portion of its already diminished military capacity, preventing these prisoners from joining the war effort against the Soviet Union (Snyder, 2010). Fischer (2007) has stated that "the NKVD eliminated almost half the Polish officer corps". The extermination of the cultural élite was also a key objective to hinder any future offensive action.

Katyń is one of three execution and burial sites. The Katyń site was specifically used for the Poles interned at the Kozielsk camp (Figure 1). Those interned at the Starobielsk site were taken to the Kharkov prison, executed and buried at Plati-chatki, while those held at Ostaszków were executed in the Kalinin prison and buried at Miednoje. With the remaining 7000 prisoners executed at sites like Charków, the name Katyń has become an umbrella term for the entire massacre.

Prior to their execution, prisoners had been in (censored) correspondence with their families who knew where they were and who their captors were (Paul, 1991). Following their execution, enquiries made by the families as to their relatives' whereabouts were met with silence. The prisoners were mostly buried in uniform in prepared trenches with a variety of "personal papers, documents, letters" still on their person (Lauck, 1988; Sanford, 2005, p. 33). These documents, together with the timing of their execution in spring 1940, which influenced the rate of decomposition, meant that it was clear that the Soviets had controlled the Katyń territory at the time of the executions.[2]

Establishing and Reinforcing Absence

The Katyń story has derived much of its potency from the construction and main-tenance of an absent narrative. The Soviet Union played the largest role in main-taining the silence around Katyń, as well as influencing others' decisions to participate in this silence. In the following sections, I detail key moments in the Katyń story, which demonstrate how an enforced absence of public narratives of Katyń has strengthened and sustained these narratives in private spheres.

The first significant occurrence in the Katyń story after the massacre was the launch of 'Operation Barbarosa' on 30 July 1941. This action signalled the Wer-macht's advance eastward and the breaking of the original Soviet–German alli-ance recorded in the Molotov–Ribbentrop Pact. With the dissolution of this alliance, the Soviet Union was now fighting a common enemy with the Allies and was obliged to issue an amnesty to all Polish persons "deprived of their freedom on the territory of the USSR" (Lauck, 1988; Sanford, 2006, p. 99). This amnesty was effected on 12 August 1941. The Polish government-in-exile in London was eager to re-establish a Polish Military Mission in Russia under General Władysław Anders and consequently queried the location of their 320 000 deported citizens and the military officers.

A key first step in the re-establishment of diplomatic relations was providing the Polish government-in-exile with a list of former detainees. Of those listed, some 10 000 military personnel were missing—namely, those who were known to have been interned at Ostaszków, Kozielsk and Starobielsk (Zaslavsky, 2009, p. 89). Two Polish envoys to the Kremlin (on 7 October 1941 and 14 October

1941) sought to ascertain the fate of the missing soldiers. Both envoys were unsuccessful, although by the latter the Soviets had established their position that all Polish officers had been released, or would soon be freed (Zaslavsky, 2009, p. 88). Once this position was established, Stalin went to lengths to maintain it. For example, Sanford (2006, p. 101) has cited one instance in November 1941 of Stalin pretending to call the NKVD in the presence of Polish diplomat Stanisław Kot, asking them if all the Poles had already been released. In subsequent questioning in December 1941, Stalin infamously claimed that those that had not been freed had escaped to Manchuria (Lauck, 1988).

This Soviet-induced silence was indeed political; Stalin and the Allies had a mutually self-servicing relationship. As the war progressed, the Allies' reliance on the Soviet Union as part of the war effort, and on maintenance of the eastern front, meant that the UK was not willing to risk offending the Soviet Poltiburo by pursuing Polish requests to investigate the matter further. From this early stage, the Soviets and the Allies chose not to 'select' or publicise the Katyń memory. Indeed, they decreed that Katyń be selectively 'forgotten' (Zaslavsky, 2009). The threat to political legitimacy and control of territory were drivers for the removal and stifling of this memory in the public sphere.

Yet, the Katyń memory could not be suppressed. On 11 April 1943, the German Army announced the discovery of mass graves in the Katyń Forest. However, Cienciala and Materski (2007) have argued that the Germans knew about the graves as early as summer 1942, while Sanford (2006) has suggested winter 1942. Nonetheless, from July 1941, the Germans occupied the region around Katyń, establishing a regimental headquarters near to the Katyń Forest (Cienciala and Materski, 2007). The Germans purposefully used their ability to (re)introduce the Katyń narrative in the public sphere to test the relationship between the London Poles and their Allies (Cienciala and Materski, 2007; Sanford, 2005), but also to establish a coverup for the liquidation of the Warsaw ghetto. By choosing when to publicise their discovery, the Germans intended to give the Allies a glimpse of the Politburo's ultimate plans for Eastern Europe and developed propaganda material to support this viewpoint.

The (re)surfacing of news of Katyń via the German press release presented an intriguing example of how two powerful wartime opponents moved between suppressing and exposing the memory narrative for their own political advantages. Both the Germans and the Soviets were using Katyń to destabilise the existing relationship between the London-based Poles and the Allies. The Polish government, "under [internal Polish] pressure to take a stand" requested an official investigation by the International Red Cross (Cienciala and Materski, 2007, p. 217). A concurrent German request for a Red Cross investigation was 'used' by the Soviets to insinuate a "co-ordinated conspiracy" between the Poles and the Germans (Sanford, 2005, p. 129). Part of the Polish Red Cross delegation comprised Polish resistance members who, after independently determining Soviet guilt, were reticent to publish their conclusions for fear of inflaming both Nazi and Soviet propaganda (Zaslavsky, 2009, pp. 91–92). Instead, they provided the British government with the only copy. As part of the Allied governments' role in silencing Katyń, the document was hidden for 45 years and only published in 1989 (Zaslavsky, 2009, p. 92).

The Soviet denial of Katyń served to unhinge the existing relationship between the Polish government-in-exile and their London allies. Eventually, this fracture would influence decisions on post-WWII Polish territory and the positioning of the Curzon Line, decided at Yalta by Churchill, Roosevelt and Stalin. The Soviet silence was both imposed and supported by Churchill and Roosevelt. Churchill's support of Stalin's propaganda was based on the belief that any German involvement in the investigation of the massacre would render it fraudulent (Sanford, 2005) and part of a "futile attempt by Germany to postpone defeat by political methods" (Zaslavsky, 2009, p. 95). Further, Churchill prohibited the circulation of a memorandum expounding Soviet guilt. Similarly, in 1945, Roosevelt forbade the publication of 'unfavourable' material concerning Katyń as it would implicate an important ally (Zaslavsky, 2009, p. 95). The Polish persistence in lobbying with the UK government to investigate Katyń was not viewed favourably in the wartime climate given the dependency upon the Soviets in maintaining the Eastern front. Despite continued Polish efforts, the Katyń story faded from the spotlight until the end of the war.

The Effects of the Post-WWII Silence

After WWII, access to information about Katyń became even more strictly controlled by the Soviet-led Polish government. Katyń became taboo; reference to it disappeared from Soviet publications, encyclopaedias, maps and classrooms. Reference was only ever made to the Burdenko version—Burdenko was the head of the second international, but Soviet-led, delegation to Katyń. This Soviet version forged an alternative narrative of Katyń based on German guilt. Within the Burdenko version, German guilt was premised on the bullets being German in origin. The Soviets used memory as a "rather useful" tool to dictate what was present in public discourse and, indeed, what was purposefully forgotten and silenced (Said, 2000, p. 179). Post-WWII, the cultural memories of the Polish nation were once again dominated by a powerful hegemon. While Poles who had family members at Katyń would have had strong suspicions of Soviet responsibility, citizens and the nation were never able to mourn the loss of these lives openly. Moreover, the public condemnation of the perpetrators was impossible—they were now brothers in Socialism. The Soviet regime controlled the Katyń memory by establishing a fear of recrimination through force by threatening imprisonment and exile. The implication of this level of control meant that they could also control the narrative without force, because the fear of recrimination acted to reinforce the silencing and the regime's alternate narrative. Reflecting on revolutions, dictatorships and other turbulent events in the mid 20th century in African nations, Kapuściński has contended

> No one defends the maker of a loud noise, whereas those who establish silence in their own states are protected by an apparatus of repression. That is why the battle against silence is so difficult (Kapuściński, 1986, p. 190).

The political mobilisation of memory meant that memory was spirited in private (and safer) spheres, in particular to the family where it could be (more) openly discussed. Till (1999, p. 265) has argued that Socialist societies were not structured by the same public/private dichotomy as Western societies but by state/family arenas. The effect of this dichotomy meant that, unlike their counterparts in non-Socialist societies, Poles (and others in Socialist countries) did not have the same ability to access or discuss information in the public sphere, as information and the media were strictly controlled by the state. In private spheres, the family was left as both the only trusted source of and space for alternative information and discussion. Halbwachs (1926/1992) has classified the family as a distinct social framework for the construction, transmission and preservation of memories. While the family commonly acts as a distinct sphere of memory, in post-war Poland, this function was made all the more important because the absence of a public narrative compelled its presence in private spheres. The family became a private and confidential place, not only to grieve and to express other emotions, but also to remember and to educate children of an alternate historical narrative not possible in the public sphere. As Orla-Bukowska (2006) and Till (1999, p. 265) have noted, "open discussion took place behind closed doors (and at personal risk) with family members over the kitchen tables".

The effect of the public suppression of Katyń memories was evident in a group of post-Socialist migrants who had lived in Poland and migrated between the 1980s and 1990s. These migrants had experienced the absence of public Katyń memories first hand. Yet this did not necessarily mean that they all discussed or remembered Katyń within their private spheres. Rather, they were polarised as to whether it was possible even to know about Katyń during the Socialist period in Poland. Those who knew about Katyń thought that everybody knew about it

> Everybody knew about it ... At home we were [told about] what happened in Katyń (Respondent 11, 21 July 2006).

> I knew about it, [Katyń]. Everyone knew and this was like officially [it] didn't happen. And then everyone was saying you know this happened and the Polish officers were killed and Polish intelligence [too]. This was ... [in the] years that Russia was our greatest friend/greatest enemy (Respondent 19, 2 August 2006).

While Poles saw the passing-on of an alternate history in the family home as an accepted outcome of the public suppression of national memory, one could only pass on a memory of Katyń if one had knowledge of it in the first place. The enforced public silence about the massacre meant that there was no possible safe way of confirming that everyone did indeed know about it, because people would not talk about it outside trusted circles. For example, one participant commented

> Our parents were very careful not to tell us about it until we were mature enough to understand that you immediately forget it, in terms of not talking about it in public, because then they could be in trouble (Respondent 58, 21 June 2006).

In contrast, some of the participants (six of the14 post-Socialist migrants) only found out about Katyń after they migrated to Australia

> I learn[ed] about Katyń ... in [the] '90s in Solidarity, when people started to talk about it (Respondent 68, 1 July 2006).

> [Katyń] wasn't told at all. Like because we didn't read outside [Poland] ... Maybe my parents didn't know about Katyń (Respondent 18, 26 July 2006).

But Katyń was not something that was talked about in the early '70s, not many people knew about. I think it ... was exposed later, 'cause I've learnt about it while living in Australia (Respondent 4, 17 July 2006).

Most striking was the sense of disbelief among these participants that they did not know about Katyń. This lack of awareness reinforces the effectiveness of the Soviet dissimulation of the Katyń memories. The suppression resulted in two forms of 'naturalness' and 'normality' about Katyń narratives. First, those who did not know were generally convinced after the fact that nobody knew—it was the norm not to know. Secondly, for those who knew about Katyń, it felt normal to know and normal not to discuss the matter beyond the private sphere of the family. Kapuściński articulates this interrelationship between power and silence

For a while it does indeed look as if they can do whatever they want. Scandal after scandal and illegality after illegality go unpunished. The people remain silent ... They are afraid and do not yet feel their own strength (Kapuściński, 1982, p. 190).

Public control of the narrative meant that it was rare (for fear of imprisonment) that these two groups communicated.

Public Memory Transfer Post-Socialism

As time passed, opposition to the silence grew louder. Through the late 1970s, the Gierek government "did little to clamp down on... [those] who propagated the Katyń theme" (Sanford, 2005, p. 195). Katyń was one of many symbolic issues that workers campaigned about during the emergence of Solidarność (the Polish Independent Self-governing Trade Union) and in the strikes at the Gdańsk shipyards during the 1980s (Kubik, 1994). Meanwhile, the Soviet government tried to maintain control of the memory. A propagandist memorial erected in a small village in Belarus with a similar name, Khatyn,[3] received widespread attention when visited by President Richard Nixon in 1974 (Sanford, 2005). Yet, the coverup extended in the face of the mounting pressure from the Solidarity strikes. In 1981, a memorial with the inscription 'Katyń 1940', erected in Warsaw by Solidarność was hastily removed and substituted, under Russian direction, with a memorial that read: "To the Polish soldiers—victims of Hitlerite fascism—reposing in the soil of Katyń" (Fischer, 2007).

Having known about Katyń prior to 1990, on April 13, Gorbachev began a process of conciliation to investigate 'blank spots' in Polish/Soviet memory (Fischer, 2007; Sanford, 2005; Zaslavsky, 2009, p. 71). Two folders were handed to the Polish President Wojciech Jaruzelski. These provided an incomplete list of 14 793 victims and they started a process of documentation and access of official records to the Polish government. Yet crucially absent from the folder were the actual execution orders, signed by Stalin. Fischer (2007) has argued that this was a politically strategic move by Gorbachev, who then directed blame for the massacre towards Beria only, who had been discredited and executed by Stalin's successors. In October 1992, Boris Yeltsin handed the execution orders and 42 other documents to the new democratically elected Polish President Lech Wałęsa.

The surfacing of the Katyń narrative and the Soviet acknowledgement of responsibility opened up two distinct realms of public commemoration, one providing the opportunity for public discussion about the massacre, the other enabling its memorialisation. In 1990, one such memorial was erected in

Kraków (Figure 2), located at the end of the Royal Way on *ul. Grodzka,* adjacent to the Wawel Castle—an important cultural site and major tourist attraction. The choice of this location also demonstrates the ability of the newly elected democratic government to control the narrative and position the memorial in a highly traversed public space. A discursive reading of the memorial revealed a distinctly post-Socialist commemorative 'approach'. Despite the monument's location—adjacent to a popular tourist site—it is specifically designed for Polish audiences only. The plaque at the foot of the monument references places of Soviet aggression towards Poles during and after WWII: Kolziesk, Ostaszków and Starobielsk are listed here on the top line (Figure 2). These places are unambiguous to a Polish audience: they link Soviet aggression to narratives of Polish cultural memory. There is no further information (translated or otherwise) near the monument, possibly because the monument, while a long-awaited public manifestation of cultural memory, is intended to reference the years of silence and acknowledge and reinforce the on-going strength of private memory.

Through its form, the monument contributes to the Polish narrative of suffering and struggle. The cross is a widely recognised symbol of Christianity and of suffering and crucifixion. Kubik (1994) has argued that in Poland the symbol of the cross has three additional meanings. First, "it was a sign of defiance towards the Communist regime", which was secular (Kubik, 1994, p. 189). Secondly, "it was metaphor of national martyrdom". Thirdly, "it was a symbol of Poland as the Messiah of nations". By using a cross to memorialise the Katyń massacre, the audience is provided with a context in which to remember this macabre

Figure 2. Katyń cross memorial, Kraków, Poland. *Source*: Author's photograph.

event—within the historical and Catholic narrative of Polish suffering. The cross holds the memory of the victims of Katyń *and* the memory of Poland's tribulations under its Soviet oppressors, referenced in the place names listed on the plaque. Yet, in choosing this Christian form of commemoration, the memorial silences other non-Christian memories of Katyń. Snyder (2010) has quoted Swianiewicz's (2002) *W Cieniu Katynia* (In the Shadow of Katyń), an eyewitness account, to estimate that about 8 per cent of those executed were Jewish and that other non-Poles such as Ukrainians and Belarusians were also among the dead. The power of selection in the memory landscape is not always inclusive, even when wielded by non-totalitarian governments or in non-totalitarian environments.

Post-Socialism, a politics of memory has continued to influence (re)productions of Katyń memories within private spheres. With Katyń monuments now performing this memory-work in public and, as in the aforementioned example, providing the commemorative context too, has the obligation for private memory transfer diminished given the narrative's public presence? As Young (1993, p. 5) has contended, "we encourage monuments to do our memory-work for us, we become that much more forgetful". An intriguing parallel situation appears to be evident in the Polish Australian diaspora, where post-Socialism, the ability publicly to discuss Katyń, seems to have dissolved the personal onus to transmit the memory privately. In Poland, suppression had created active resistance (and a greater sense of personal responsibility). However, allowed public discussion, which in practice would have mainly taken place intragenerationally, seems to have replaced the practice of intergenerational memory transfer. This process is overlain with the extra complexities of being in diaspora, which despite the pre-eminence of the Katyń case to the Polish identity narrative, is presumably also affected by a weakening of cultural identities.

Such a shift in the onus of memory-work was evident in a cohort of second-generation post-Socialist migrants to Australia. This cohort were children of people who had experienced the absence of Katyń memories in post-WWII Poland.[4] Only six of the 14 second-generation participants knew about Katyń. Of these participants, two indicated that they had learned about Katyń during school history lessons, not from home. The remaining eight participants had no, or very vague, knowledge of the massacre. While this might suggest that Katyń has not been considered an important cultural memory to pass on, several post-Socialist participants (the parents of the second generation) stressed the difficulty in discussing their experiences during the Soviet occupation with their children. For example

> No I don't say it's not important—it's very important—but I don't think that they would be able to understand it. It is just a completely different world . . . [a] distorted picture of humanity (Respondent 11, 21 July 2006).

> The whole communist era is such an abuse of human rights, but they [my children] can't understand. It's almost impossible to translate, to explain to my daughter . . . the stupidity of things that happened there. It was, like, surreal. We lived in it, so we adapted, but if you just went, thrown into it, you couldn't understand anything, 'cause everything was on two levels at least: the official level and the sort of popular level (Respondent 58, 21 June 2006).

It is intriguing that even when geographically removed from the environment of suppression—in diaspora in Australia—and nearly two decades later, there is a lasting impact of how the silencing of Katyń influences the passing on of cultural memory and, indeed, perpetuates some of those original silences.[5]

The New Katyń Terrain

On 10 April 2010, a new scar was etched over the Katyń narrative. A plane carrying the president and 95 other Poles—military, heads of government departments, and other dignitaries—crashed en route to a Katyń memorial service near Smolensk, Russia. Almost instantly, comparisons were drawn between the 1940 and 2010 events—in terms of their location, Russian involvement and the large numbers of high-ranking officials who perished in both events. Yet this time there was no enforced suppression of the news of the crash. Details emerged almost spontaneously and on an international stage.

The political terrain that followed the crash was inextricably linked to the preceding internal politics regarding the memorialisation of Katyń and Polish–Russian relations more generally (Nowak, 2011). President Kaczyński and Premier Tusk were from opposing political parties[6] and their opinions about Poland's political positioning and its ability to move forward from an unfortunate past were widely divergent. As Nowak (2011) has explained, the Kaczyńskis were defiant in their reluctance to reconcile with their eastern neighbour, citing a long and recent history of oppression as justification.

A critical element of the story of Katyń in 2010 was that President Kaczyński had organised an alternate trip to commemorate Katyń on his own accord. Premier Tusk's had occurred three days prior at the invitation of the Russian Prime Minister Vladimir Putin but Kaczyński had not been invited. The invitation of Premier Tusk had been widely viewed as a step forward in Polish–Russian relations. Yet, Putin had fallen short of an apology, instead referencing Katyń as the location where both Russians and Poles had died at the hands of Stalin, as victims of totalitarianism (Szonert, 2010).

Nowak (2011, p. 3) has also argued that Kaczyński specially organised Katyń commemorations to pay tribute to the victims, but also to "remind the world that an ideology that tries to rehabilitate the crimes of Stalinism ... could be dangerous and detrimental". Tusk, on the other hand, saw a necessity in breaking free from "canonical elements of Polish victimhood [and] self-sacrifice" (Nowak, 2011, p. 2). In 2009, in a move to reconcile Polish–Russian relations, Tusk invited Putin to participate in the anniversary of WWII Westerplatte, the location where the first offensive action of WWII by the German army was launched on a Polish naval facility, and then on the adjoining city of Gdańsk. After the crash, Katyń's resonance with the politics of memory thematic continued. Presidential elections scheduled for October 2010 needed to be brought forward; the President's party (PiS) had been widely predicted to face an electoral defeat before the plane crash. Questions had been asked whether the party's strong nationalistic sentiments and its dogged championing of a Polish narrative of suffering under occupation was counter-productive to Poland's ability to move forward in the European Union. According to Nowak (2011), it was (in part) the continuing associations with narratives of martyrdom and victimhood that cost Kaczyński's party the election. The elections were held amid national mourning, but also among the added political and media controversy of the deceased President's burial in the Wawel cathedral, in Kraków, beside past monarchs, poets and revolutionaries. Meanwhile, shortly after the crash, and in what could be interpreted as a 'conciliatory gesture' (Szonert-Binienda, 2012), the Russian government made public for the first time documents relating to the 1940 massacre, including the signed execution orders—previously only available to a select group of researchers. Similarly, after the crash, the "Russian Supreme Court ordered the Moscow City Court to consider an appeal by the Polish group '*Memoriał*' to declassify the decision of Russian military prosecutors to close the Katyń investigation" (Gorska, 2010). Yet, Szonert-Binienda (2012) has argued that, despite an apparent show of goodwill through the release of documents and gestures, the legal treatment of Katyń in the Russian courts remains unchanged—Katyń remains classified as a crime of 'exceeding official authority'.

'A Permanent Scar on [Our] Memory?'

While knowledge of Katyń continues to be made public, and investigations into both the 1940 and 2010 events continue, many unanswered questions remain. Only in November 2011 did the Russian Duma formally acknowledge Katyń as a crime specifically ordered by Stalin. As this (albeit) brief overview of the recent politics has demonstrated, the commemoration of Katyń was still highly political within Polish post-Socialist politics, even up until the recent plane crash. Indeed, the historical shifting of the Katyń narrative between public absence and presence has only fuelled deep-seated nationalistic sentiments and suspicions about the investigations into the recent tragedy. Because Russia, as historical perpetrator, will always be part of the Katyń story, moving on from a besieged past narrative presents many challenges.

The 2010 crash raised the profile of the massacre internationally, but also within Russian society and media, which have been grappling with public discourse about Stalinist and Communist-era crimes (Gorska, 2010; Nowak, 2011). The screening in Russia of Andrzej Wajda's *Katyń* (2007), before and after the crash, demonstrated some readiness to make the Katyń story accessible to the general Russian public. Polish–Russian relations again received international exposure at the 2011 memorial ceremony for the plane crash victims. The relatives of the victims had previously affixed a memorial plaque to a cross indicating that Kaczyński and others had died en route to commemorate "the Soviet crime of genocide against prisoners of war, Polish Army officers" (Kramer, 2011). Yet, this plaque was removed and replaced in Russian and Polish with, "in memory of 96 Poles led by the president of the Republic of Poland, Lech Kaczynski, who died in a plane crash near Smolensk on April 10 2010". The recent removal of the plaque in Smolensk was strikingly similar to the removal of the monument in Warsaw 1981. In both instances, the rewording has suppressed the issuance of blame towards the Russian nation from the public sphere. Despite the passage of time and some progress at overcoming historical barriers, it would seem that processes of conciliation remain protracted and contentious and, as Poland's First Lady, Anna Komorowska has contended, a "permanent scar" on Polish memory.

After the most recent Katyń tragedy, Poles were able actively and publicly to commemorate the 96 victims, in a way not possible for the previous tragedy before the fall of communism. The on-going prevalence of Katyń in the media and within public discourse suggests that perhaps Poles are still catching up with their open grief (of both events), on a public stage. The plane crash also had the effect of internationalising the knowledge of the massacre and the original tragedy. News of the plane crash was broadcast internationally within minutes. Contextualising these news stories were open references to the original massacre and the political coverup. The contrast in the way that the 1940 and 2010 events were both nationally and internationally broadcast exemplifies how a politics of memory changes with both time and context. Because Katyń's former taboo status—both internationally and in Poland—was imposed by Russia, the obligation to remember became tightly interweaved with narratives of suffering and struggle of the Polish nation, epitomised by Soviet aggression and dominance. Despite attempts to move forward from these entrenched identities, the most recent tragedy has given them new voice but also increased discussion, further complicating an already complex Katyń story.

Notes

1. For a detailed description and analysis of the massacre see Sanford, 2005, 2006; Zaslavsky, 2009; IPN, 2004.
2. Lauck (1988) and Sanford (2005) have commented that fir trees were also planted over the burial sites; these were younger in age and differ in coverage to adjoining forested areas.
3. Khatyn was one of 136 Belarusian villages where all inhabitants were killed by the Nazis during WWII (Sanford, 2005).
4. The majority were born in Australia, with a few migrating as children under five years of age.
5. These research interviews were conducted in 2006 prior to the recent plane crash in 2010. It is probable that, were the interviews conducted in the present-day, this cohort would now be aware of Katyń, because the recent plane crash has reasserted the importance of the Katyń narrative internationally.
6. Kaczyński's twin Jarosław headed Prawo i Sprawiedliwość (PiS, Law and Justice Party), while Tusk is chairman of Platforma Obywatelska (PO, Civic Platform).

References

ALLBROOK, M. and CATTALINI, H. (1995) *The General Langfitt Story: Polish Refugees Recount Their Experiences of Exile, Dispersal and Resettlement.* Canberra: Australian Government Publishing Service.

ARGENBRIGHT, R. (1999) Remaking Moscow: new places, new selves, *Geographical Review*, 89, pp. 1–22.

BURLEIGH, M. (1988) *Germany Turns Eastwards: A Study of Ostforschung in the Third Reich.* Cambridge: Cambridge University Press.

CIENCIALA, A. M. and MATERSKI, W. (2007) *Katyń: A Crime without Punishment.* New York: Yale University Press.

DROZDZEWSKI, D. (2008) *Remembering Polishness: Articulating and maintaining identity through turbulent times.* Unpublished PhD Thesis, University of New South Wales, Australia.

DUNCAN, J. S. (1990) *The City as Text: The Politics of Landscape Interpretation in the Kanydan Kingdom.* Cambridge: Cambridge University Press.

DUNN, K. M. (2004) Islam in Sydney: contesting the discourse of absence, *Australian Geographer*, 35, pp. 333–353.

EDKINS, J. (2003) *Trauma and the Memory of Politics.* Cambridge: Cambridge University Press.

ESBENSHADE, R. S. (1995) Remembering to forget: memory, history, national identity in postwar east-central Europe, *Representations*, 49, pp. 72–96.

FISCHER, B. B. (2007) *The Katyń controversy: Stalin's killing field* (https://www.cia.gov/library/center-for-the-study-of-intelligence/csi publications/csi-studies/studies/winter99-00/art6.html; accessed 22 September 2011).

FOOTE, K. E., TOTH, A. and ARVAY, A. (2000) Hungary after 1989: inscribing a new past on place, *Geographical Review*, 90, pp. 301–334.

FORREST, B. and JOHNSON, J. (2002) Unravelling the threads of history: Soviet-era monuments and post-Soviet national identity in Moscow, *Annals of the Association of American Geographers*, 92, pp. 524–547.

FORREST, B. and JOHNSON, J. (2011) Monumental politics: regime type and public memory in post-communist states, *Post-Soviet Affairs*, 27, pp. 269–288.

GORSKA, J. A. (2010) *Katyń: step by step gradualism* (http://rowmanblog.typepad.com/rowman/slavic_studies/; accessed 1 October 2011).

HALBWACHS, M. (1926/1992) *On Collective Memory.* Chicago, IL: University of Chicago Press.

HAY, I., HUGHES, A. and TUTTON, M. (2004) Monuments, memory and marginalisation in Adelaide's Prince Henry Gardens, *Geografiska Annaler,* 86B, pp. 201–216.

HAYDEN, D. (1995) *The Power of Place: Urban Landscapes as Public History.* Cambridge, MA: MIT Press.

HERSHKOVITZ, L. (1993) "Tiananmen Square and the politics of place", *Political Geography,* 12(5), pp. 395–420.

HOELSCHER, S. and ALDERMAN, D. (2004) Memory and place: geographies of a critical relationship, *Social and Cultural Geography,* 5, pp. 347–355.

IPN (Institute of National Remembrance) (2004) *Decision to commence investigation into Katyń massacre.* Commission for the Prosecution of Crimes against the Polish Nation, Warsaw (http://www.ipn.gov. pl/portal/en/2/77/Decision_to_commence_investigation_into_Katyn_Massacre.html; accessed 20 September 2011).

IPN (2008) *The expelled.* Exhibition, Warsaw

JOHNSON, N. (1995) Cast in stone: monuments, geography, and nationalism, *Environment and Planning D,* 13, pp. 51–65.

KAPUŚCIŃSKI, R. (1982) *The Shah of Shahs.* New York: Vintage International.

KAPUŚCIŃSKI, R. (1986) *The Soccer War.* New York: Vintage International.

KRAMER, A. E. (2011) Poland and Russia spar over wording of memorial, *New York Times,* 10 April (http://www.nytimes.com/2011/04/11/world/europe/11katyn.html; accessed 1 October 2011).

KUBIK, J. (1994) *The Power of Symbols against the Symbols of Power: The Rise of Solidarity and the Fall of State Socialism in Poland.* University Park, PA: Pennsylvania State University Press.

LAUCK, J. H. (1988) *Katyń Killings: In the Record.* Clifton, NJ: Kingston Press.

LIGHT, D., NICOLAE, I. and SUDITU, B. (2002) Toponymy and the communist city: street names in Bucharest, 1948–1965, *GeoJournal,* 56, pp. 135–144.

MITCHELL, K. (2003) Monuments, memorials, and the politics of memory, *Urban Geography,* 24, pp. 442–459.

NAGEL, C. (2002) Reconstructing space, re-creating memory: sectarian politics and urban development in post-war Beirut, *Political Geography,* 21, pp. 717–725.

NOWAK, A. (2011) From memory clashes to a general battle: the battle for Smolensk/Katyń, *East European Memory Studies,* 6, pp. 1–4.

ORLA-BUKOWSKA, A. (2006) New threads on an old loom: national memory and social identity in postwar and post-Communist Poland, in: R. N. LEBOW, W. KANSTEINER and C. FOGU (Eds) *The Politics of Memory in Postwar Europe,* pp. 177–209. Durham, NC: Duke University Press.

PAUL, A. (1991) *Katyń: Stalin's Massacre and the Seeds of Polish Resurrection.* Anapolis, MD: Naval Institute Press.

SAID, E. W. (2000) Invention, memory and place, *Critical Inquiry,* 26, pp. 175–192.

SANFORD, G. (2005) *Katyń and the Soviet Massacre of 1940.* London: Routledge.

SANFORD, G. (2006) The Katyń massacre and Polish-Soviet relations, 1941–43, *Journal of Contemporary History,* 41, pp. 95–111.

SARGIN, G. A. (2004) Displaced memories, or the architecture of forgetting and remembrance, *Environment and Planning D,* 22, pp. 659–680.

SNYDER, T. (2010) *Bloodlands: Europe between Hitler and Stalin.* New York: Basic Books.

STANGL, P. (2008) The vernacular and the monumental: memory and landscape in post-war Berlin, *GeoJournal,* 73, pp. 213–236.

STRAEHELI, L. A. and MITCHELL, D. (2007), "Locating the public in research and practice", *Progress in Human Geography,* 31(6), pp. 792–811.

SWIANIEWICZ, W. (2002) *W Cieniu Katynia* [In the Shadow of Katyń]. Warsaw: Czytelnik.

SZONERT, M. (2010) The 'Katyń' plane crash, *Polonia News Magazine,* 10 April (http://www. polonianewsmagazine.com/MS04-2010-060.html; accessed 1 October 2011).

SZONERT-BINIENDA, M. (2012) *Was Katyń a genocide?* Working Paper, Case Western Reserve Journal of International Law (http://www.case.edu/orgs/jil/Katyn_Conference_Papers/Szonert-Was_ Katyn_a_Genocide.pdf; accessed 29 June 2012).

TILL, K. E. (1999) Staging the past: landscape designs, cultural identity and *Erinnerungspolitik* at Berlin's Neue Wache, *Ecumene,* 6, pp. 251–283.

YOUNG, J. E. (1993) *Texture of Memory Holocaust Memorials and Meaning.* Newhaven, CT: Yale University Press.

ZASLAVSKY, V. (2009) *The Katyń Massacre: 'Class Cleansing' as Totalitarian Praxis.* New York: Telos Press.

Criminals with 'Community Spirit': Practising Citizenship in the Hidden World of the Prison

JENNIFER TURNER

Abstract. Contra the notion of prisons as discrete, 'hidden' spaces, contemporary research has stressed a range of connections, transactions and exchange. The relationship between the offender and the outside communities—captured in the policy rhetoric of rehabilitation and the promotion of good citizenship—is just one of these connections. This paper explores contemporary, liberal imaginations of the 'ideal' citizen; it goes on to critique formal rehabilitation programmes and highlight informal mechanisms developed within the prison environment which disrupt these constructions. Ultimately, this allows a deeper appreciation of how, despite attempts to practise citizenship in an environment that renders conventional rights and responsibilities absent, the prisoner remains altogether 'less than ideal'.

Introduction

In recent years, prisons and the penal system have come to be understood as something more than peripheral to the societies that build and populate them. Contemporary research has highlighted that there is in fact a whole range of connections, transactions and exchange that contradict perceptions of a boundary between a 'hidden' inside and the world outside (Baer and Ravneberg, 2008; Gilmore, 2007; Loyd *et al.*, 2009; Martin and Mitchelson, 2009; Pallot, 2005; Vergara, 1995; Wacquant, 2009, 2001, 2000). In this paper, I consider one such area of in-betweeness—namely, societal expectations of modern citizenship (in general) and the mechanisms via which penal authorities negotiate a particular rendering of these as they seek to create/recreate/reform 'ideal' citizens who have been subject to a penal system of punishment and rehabilitation. Using empirics drawn from a longer-term study of voluntary-work programmes for offenders, I investigate how an ensemble of societal duties such as those of good parenthood and an obligation to neighbours—as well as a formal suite of rules and regulations pertaining to good behaviour—are all visible within an environment that renders most conventional rights and responsibilities concerning citizenship absent. In highlighting what I see as tensions within the construction of a prisoner identity, I am critical of the ability of these formal mechanisms to generate individuals who remain anything other than 'less than ideal'.

Prisoners = 'Not Good Citizens'

Citizenship is a complex analytical approach as well as object of inquiry. As a critique, it is useful because it offers a tool with which to explore the "systematic discrepancies between the obligations required of and the rights extended to members of the nation-state" (Smith, 1989, p. 148). And, traditionally, the acquisition of rights associated with the granting of citizenship has been a normative expectation. Yet, as Jessop (1988) observes, contemporary society has re-evaluated citizenship to focus upon duties and obligations. Certainly in the 'Big Society' manifesto of the current British coalition government, there is a strong emphasis on the articulation of citizenship at scales beneath those of the nation-state and on the significance of locality or 'place' as a grounding for modes of citizenship based both on the assertion of individual rights *and* the appropriate performance of obligations to the community.

Scale is an important organisational mode here because the state acts to reconfigure the levels at which citizenship is defined and expected to be practised. We are moving from the concept of 'national citizens' who benefit from rights offered by managed liberalism and the welfare state, to the 'active citizen', wherein membership is imbued with responsibilities, often implemented in the local community through associations like Neighbourhood Watch (Rose, 1996). Fyfe and Milligan (2003a, 2003b) highlight how cities, neighbourhoods and other locality-based 'communities' have been envisioned as key sites for democracy and participation. This has been done both by governments seeking to *downscale* citizenship in the context of neo-liberal reforms and by groups seeking to advance particular rights, including claims over territory (Desforges *et al.*, 2005, p. 440).

Importantly for this discussion, academics have considered the significance of such things as geographical difference and global mobility, which complicate the relationship between territory and belonging. These factors have revealed emerging (re)negotiations of the normative dimensions of the meaning and practice of contemporary citizenships (Smith and Guarnizo, 2009), allowing us to consider how prisoners 'outside' any conventional territory might be included in such practices. Yet, there is a larger dynamic of exclusion; borders are rendered as imagined, particularly through discourses of fear (Pain, 2009). Similar to the identity of 'undesirable' often constructed for 'non-nationals', the prisoner is often determined as the 'other' and at a distance, metaphorical as well as physical, from the citizen majority.

Combessie (2002), for example, examines notions of good and evil manifest in the labelling and identities of officers and inmates, and the stigma that a prison can transfer beyond its walls to the outside. In a different vein, Thompson notes the paradoxical rhetorics associated with prisoners, insofar as

> The 'good citizen' is both a rhetorical object of the prison process—it is what they state they are taking the prisoner towards—and also a reference point that defines the prisoners' difference. They are labelled as *not* good citizens. The words citizen and prisoner function as a dichotomy to include and exclude (Thompson, 2000, p. 183).

Prisoners, in juxtaposition to the 'outside' citizen, default defined by the absence of some of the rights of the latter. Their fundamental loss of liberty denies their access to the rights of their peers on the outside, such as unemployment and child benefit, and limits others such as access to or choice of health service providers. As some scholars have noted, this can often have differential detrimental effects upon prisoners, tending to weigh most heavily on minority groups such as deaf prisoners (Gahir *et al.*, 2011; McCay, 2010) or those who require specialist education (Miller, 2004). Media outlets have found hot topics in contentious issues such as women in labour losing their rights to privacy and sometimes being made to give birth in chains (BBC, 2010) or the limited nature of facilities to keep children with their mothers in prison (ITV, 2011). Another notable example is the case of prisoner Martin Tate, from Caernarfon, Wales, who reported that he was not allowed to make phone calls in Welsh without giving 48 hours notice, in order that an English translator be able to listen to conversations to comply with security provisions. The Welsh Language Society deemed it 'unacceptable' and Arfon MP Hywel Williams commented that it was 'a complete injustice' (BBC, 2012). On coming out of prisons, further curtailments often continue to apply, including access to certain jobs, the ability to foster or adopt children (sentence dependent) and obtaining a mortgage or insurance (Dietrich, 2002; Metcalf *et al.*, 2001). All of these "in turn, make performing the duties of citizenship difficult" (Uggen *et al.*, 2006, p. 282).

One of the most highly contentious aspects of recent scholarly and public discussion has surrounded the consideration of whether prisoners should be prohibited from voting in elections. American Judge Dennis Challeen (1986, pp. 37–39) illustrated a glaring paradox in highlighting that, "We [the USA] want people to be responsible, so we take away all responsibility". And, scholars have noted how this issue of disenfranchisement and a 'civil death' has been a debating point since the ancient Greek and Roman times, through medieval Europe and into the present (Dhami, 2005; Ewald, 2002; Itkowitz and Oldak, 1973; Keyssar, 2000). Currently, the UK, alongside other states such as Russia, China and the US, does not allow convicted prisoners to vote. However, once released, UK prisoners—other than those convicted of treason—regain this ability. Other countries have differing legislation. For example, in Belgium, those who are incarcerated for five years or more are disenfranchised for life (Blais *et al.*, 2001). Contra this, there are member-states in the council of Europe which do already allow voting. For example, Ireland views voting in elections as part of the wider struggle for rehabilitation through normalisation (Behan and O'Donnell, 2008). In a similar vein, the Australian electoral system makes voting compulsory for those who are eligible, which includes prisoners serving a sentence of three years or less (Hill and Koch, 2011). Canada and South Africa have struggled to overturn a ban on prisoner voting, noting that their electoral commissions have no power to deny what is a deemed a 'constitutional right' (Rottinghaus and Baldwin, 2007, p. 689). Voting is a duty, it is argued, just as one's very imprisonment is recognition of the moral requirement to act in accordance with responsibilities. There is a clear recognition, clarified here especially well by Robert Patrick of the Young Foundation (n.d., n.p.) that "release from prison is not the point at which prisoners should re-engage with society. It is observed that people only experience social wealth if they believe that their voice will be heard."

UK-based organisations, such as UNLOCK, the National Association of Ex-Offenders, and the Prison Reform Trust (PRT) contest the electoral ban on sentenced prisoners voting, arguing that a reform of the law is necessary for several reasons, including the claim that a ban infringes basic human rights that people have died to protect, that it bears no relation to the causes of crime and can cause minority ethnic groups to be disenfranchised (in particular, Black men). Thus

> The notion of civic death for sentenced prisoners isolates still further those who are already on the margins of society and encourages them to be seen as alien to the communities to which they will return on release (UNLOCK, 2004, p. 1; see also Slapper, 2011).

By removing the right to vote, we signal to serving prisoners that, at least for the duration of their sentence, they are dead to society.

Bolstering such arguments are reports that disenfranchisement during incarceration has contributed to a spiral of decline of prisoners having little or no expectation to perform obligations, such as active parenthood or paying attention to financial burdens. Harman *et al.* (2007), for example, use evidence sourced from wives of incarcerated prisoners who are affronted and dismayed at the degree of free time and relaxation that their male partners enjoy when in prison, at precisely the time when they are having to manage both the family finances and the children themselves. Furthermore, May and Woods (2005) demonstrate that many American prisoners would prefer to go to prison than do community service, house arrest or 'boot camp' when offered the choice.

However, as Baer intimates, although "the confinement of prisoners hides their daily lives from most of society", that "hiddenness does not mean that their experiences are inconsequential. Prisons form their own complex cultures that are interwoven into and through the rest of society" (Baer, 2005, pp. 209–210). Thus, I use the remainder of the paper to illustrate the case of the prisoner as one which offers a vantage-point upon the demands of citizenship in general, from the perspective of those 'less than ideal' citizens existing at the boundary between the prison and society. To do this, I bring to light some of the schemes designed to rehabilitate prisoners in the UK, and the expectations regarding obligations to a larger community therein. In offering examples of these, I critique the implementation of systems designed to enfranchise prisoners with a sense of belonging or 'citizenship' to the so-called outside community, despite their physical absence from it. My analysis reveals a paradoxical situation where, despite an intent to generate a sense of duties and obligations, the prisoner continues to be positioned as altogether 'less than ideal', a subjective identity that, moreover, inflects their perception of themselves.

Constructing the Prisoner as Citizen

Focusing on the development of the responsible citizen, Burchell provides a lucid account of an attentiveness towards

> the promotion in the governed population of specific techniques of the self around such questions as, for example, saving and 'providentialism', the acquisition of ways of performing roles like father or mother, the development of habits of cleanliness, sobriety, fidelity, self-improvement, responsibility and so on (1996, p. 25).

And, Rose describes an ensuing paradoxical situation, wherein detention has been used to confine members of society who detract from the ideal, even though these 'incorrigible individuals' are then supposed to conform to the concept of the responsible, modern citizen. Rehabilitation strategies used in order to create this condition, he argues, are a form of "work experience" in this regard (Rose, 2000, p. 330). The intent here is to "remoralize" and "responsibilize" individuals such that they are able to work without benefit and further support: in short, "to reconstruct self-reliance in those who are excluded" (Rose, p. 334).

With this in mind, I developed a research agenda that focused upon rehabilitative strategies directed towards UK prisoners and ex-offenders both during and after their imprisonment. In England and Wales, this may involve inclusion on one or more of the 47 accredited Offender Behaviour Programmes (OBPs) on offer, which focus on reducing reoffending. Based on evidence from the 'What Works' literature, these programmes vary in length, complexity and mode of delivery. In the year 2010/11, there were 8981 OBP and Sex Offender Treatment Programme (SOTP) completions, from a year-end average prison population of 84 920 (Ministry of Justice, 2011, n.p.). This represents an 86 per cent achievement of the targeted number of completions (NOMS, 2011). Alongside these courses, different institutions may offer additional opportunities specific to the prison security category and/or in partnership with external charities or other organisations. Participation is "targeted according to risk and need" (Ministry of Justice, 2012, n.p.); and may be subject to further eligibility requirements.

In terms of empirical case studies, I looked at OBPs such as the Thinking Skills Programme (TSP), Focus on Resettlement (FOR) and Short Duration Programme (SDP), which are run in prisons such as Her Majesty's Prison (HMP) Hull, HMP Lindholme and HMP Newhall.[1] Other, work-based projects that I looked at include prisoners employed at *The Clink* public restaurant at HMP High Down, and the Oxford Citizen's Advice Bureau, amongst others. Observations and/or interviews with facilitators and participants (undertaken according to UK Research Council ethical considerations, and restricted access) were conducted at these sites, alongside an analysis of prisoner blogs and narratives, media outputs and ethnographies as part of a wider research project on carceral geographies.

Formal mechanisms and associated rhetorics developed as part of strategies to decrease the level of recidivism make clear that the goal is to help individuals meet the expectations of good citizenry, including a respect and tolerance for others. Characteristics outlined in directives such as Race Equality for Staff and Prisoners (RESPOND) include "eliminating all forms of discrimination within the Service" (ODPM, 2002, p. 152); and the Challenge to Change programme, which promotes a development of "positive social skills, mutual respect for others and renewed trust in society" (Kainos Community 2012, n.p.).

And, interviews with those responsible for running these confirmed such goals. According to a facilitator at HMP Newhall, for example, skills-based and self-development courses

> can improve the relationships between staff and prisoners, especially officers. This is usually as their assumptions are proved incorrect and they see a different side to officers. The course is quite intense and there needs to be a balance of trust between prisoners and staff and prisoners and prisoners (Interviewee F25SP, 29 March 2011).

Community spirit is a symbiotic skill facilitated through participation in these programmes. However, a fundamental constraint on such efforts is the emotional, as well as physical distancing of friends and family of the prisoner. As one of my interviews highlighted

> *Psychologist*: The programmes have reviews whereby they can invite family members/friends to them. I think this is very important so that parents/friends are aware of what risk factors the offender has and they can help them look out for them and prevent them. Unfortunately, in my establishment offenders do not usually want to invite family/ friends, either because it is too far to travel for them or they do not think they will want to come (Interviewee F25SP, 29 March 2011).

At HMP Durham, 'better father' workshops have been developed whereby prisoners can see their children. And, HMP Dartmoor has also addressed spatial problems such as the distance families must travel to Category A prisons (those which house offenders with the highest likelihood of escape and have limited visitation rights). Here, technological innovations have allowed the scheme StoryBook Dads to produce over 5000 CDs and DVDs in 2010 of fathers in prison recording bedtime stories and incorporating personal messages for their children. An example drawn from the StoryBook Dads website sounds

> Well Maisy, I hope you enjoyed that story. It was the story of a little princess just like you're my little princess who I miss every day. I want you to remember that Daddy's always thinking about you and I hope one day soon that I'll be able to read you this story myself and tuck you in at night. Be good for Mummy. You're always on my mind. Bye-bye! (personal message at the end of story, transcript, StoryBook Dads, 2012).

Currently, 90 other prisons take part by recording their stories and sending them to Dartmoor where they are edited and returned for the nominal cost of the postage. There is also StoryBook Mums. StoryBook Soldiers has now been set up following the Dartmoor template and is open to all the British Forces. According to proponents, schemes like this return a fundamental human right of familial interaction for prisoners and also allow them to participate in some of the responsibilities of parenthood. It can also, of course, enhance the wellbeing of children

> I miss my Dad so much. When I feel lonely I listen to my CD and hearing his voice makes me feel better (Chloe, age 7, StoryBook Dads, 2012).

The idea of participating in otherwise 'outside' activities can also be manifest in more concrete examples. The Oxford Citizens Advice Bureau (OxCAB), for example, developed the idea of training serving prisoners to become volunteer citizens' advisers in order to increase capacity and meet growing demand. The Citizens Advice Bureau (CAB) delivers advice services from over 3500 community locations in England and Wales, run by 382 individual charities. The membership organisation of the bureau is run by Citizens Advice, which is itself a registered charity. Following much debate, prisoners at HMP Springhill are now able to become Citizen Advisers. Springhill is one of the country's 12 category D open prisons, to which male prisoners at the lowest level of risk are allocated. It does not take sex offenders or arsonists. Owing to the fact that people who visit the Citizens Advice Bureau are also, often, vulnerable members of society, the selection of prisoners is rigorous and they must comply with certain eligibility requirements. At a focus group with prisoner-advisers and a facilitator, members commented

Liam: We know the sort of process you have to come through, you don't just let any old Joe Bloggs come here ... prison is full of ....
Ian: Piss takers!
Liam: You know what sort of people are in prison and ...
Oliver: Yeah, the thing is, before we even get to see [a CAB interviewer] we have to go through a rigorous risk assessment like, from the prison side of things.
Facilitator: They have to do this more than any other ... they risk access on the suitability of coming out and working with vulnerable people.
Oliver: It's more rigorous than any other project.
(Focus group 2, 12 January 2012).[2]

Alongside other volunteer advisors, their training and performance monitoring is on-going. Most prisoners complete the training within 6–8 weeks—more quickly than most other volunteers as the prisoners are available on a full-time basis. Furthermore, as prisoner-volunteers typically work four times as many hours, the OxCAB can now give advice to many more people than ever before.

The CAB aims to equip people with the knowledge required to deal with any problems they face, as well as endeavouring to shape the way policies influence daily lives. According to the Citizens Advice service, their service provides "free, independent, confidential and impartial advice to everyone on their rights and responsibilities" (2012, n.p.). It is interesting that in this case, then, the CAB is staffed by less-than-ideal citizens. And, interviewees spoke about the development of their personal knowledge database as a result of their work experience, particularly their ability to find sources of support and information for themselves following future release. Facilitators explained scenarios where prisoner-advisers had been asked to help with form-filling and make suggestions about appropriate organisations for their fellow inmates. In this respect, it can be argued that, this turns the CAB itself into a training ground, both in terms of the users and the prisoner-advisers themselves.

Although the OxCAB–Springhill partnership was originally developed to aid the Bureau rather than act as a rehabilitation project, prisoners have found many benefits in their preparation for release. For the prisoners interviewed, certainly, work at the CAB was very different from anything they had ever done before: their role gave them a sense of normality and social inclusion. A comparison was sometimes made with this "intellectually challenging" employment and "mundane" or "mediocre" jobs (repetitive and low-skilled tasks such as laundry work) that have typically been deemed appropriate for the prisoner

Liam: I've never been in this line of work ... building sites, warehouses, things like that, but ... I've now discovered ... that it is something that I enjoy doing, compared with what I was doing before, which was something that I didn't like doing ... so, yes ... I've discovered something new about myself ... I didn't think I was into this sort of thing but now, obviously, I've changed completely.
Oliver: What I like about this is here is that it's not mediocre work ... Some of the community work jobs that people do are a bit ... mundane if you like, they have to steam clothes and press, that sort of thing.

(Focus group 2, 12 January 2012).

Further to this, prisoner-advisers relished the feeling of 'fitting in' with other non-prisoner colleagues and expressed a great enjoyment at having a conventional '9 to 5' working week outside the prison environment. Indeed, the importance of achieving regular work in the future in order to provide legitimately for themselves and their families is a fundamental concern. For many prisoner-volunteers, the reference from the CAB is a major contributing factor to their decision to participate, as it goes a long way to prove their credentials to potential employers, particularly in the face of the decreased opportunities owing to their criminal record

> *Liam*: The fact that it's good for future references obviously you're going to do well to get a reference, yeah, for when you leave prison, because obviously you've got the thing of having a criminal record, coming out of prison to get a job with employers not wanting to take you on, so obviously if you've done this you've got a head start, haven't you?
> (Focus Group 2, 12 January 2012).

Brownlow (2011, p. 1271) has conceptualised citizenship as something merited or deserved, which aligns with other ideas of citizenship as a performative act that recognises and legitimises one's status within society (Lepofsky and Fraser, 2003, p. 127). As well as feeling as though they have been given the opportunity to give something back to the communities that they have been removed from, some of those involved report that the CAB work has allowed them to put their own situations into perspective, often by finding their lives to be much better than the clients they help

> *Oliver*: It is giving something back to help people who are probably, although it sounds a funny thing, even less fortunate than us who are in prison … but there are people who are in a worse position, they could be homeless, I can't imagine what that is when somebody hasn't got anywhere to sleep at night sort of thing … It makes me feel … erm … good about myself, that's the main thing, to you know, help out … that's the way I see it anyway
> *Liam*: Yeah, I definitely feel better. It sort of, redeems yourself, a bit.
> (Focus Group 2, 12 January 2012).

Prisoners are given the chance to take on a responsible role and help others—exerting their citizenship responsibilities whilst incarcerated. The Esmée Fairbairn Foundation (2004, p. 3), for example, found that CAB work "allows prisoners to retain or develop active citizenship during a period when they would otherwise be excluded from it". Isin and Nielsen (2008, p. 2) refer to these as "acts of citizenship"; that is, situations that facilitate a status that empowers people enough to be able to claim their rights as well as perform their obligations. Similar examples of projects designed to help prisoners gain a sense of 'giving something back' through purposeful endeavours includes such things as the US 'Puppies behind Bars project' where prisoners raise guide dogs for the blind (Cheakalos, 2004) and 'strengths-based' or 'restorative' activities with 'worthy causes' including repair of wheelchairs and community regeneration schemes (Burnett and Maruna, 2006) and helping the elderly (Toch, 2000). Uggen *et al.* (2004) comment upon how prisoners often feel that they can use their personal stories to prevent other people making similar mistakes.

However, these techniques can be critiqued from a number of perspectives. They are clearly intrusive, overstepping the boundary of the crime itself to allow the state to enter into a much broader moral project of reconstruction of the individual. Yet there is something more insidious here, which is the way in which even the prisoner is brought to desire their own reform. As exemplified by Liam talking about redemption (in the previous focus group excerpt), the successful functioning of these schemes requires the criminal to confess their loyalty to a market anew, articulating their aspirations to be released from prison and actively participate as a good and productive cog in the wider machine of a capitalist, liberal society. This relates to Cruikshank's (1999) Foucauldian critique of self-help initiatives, in which she argues that tools that promote empowerment, self-improvement and democratic participation are also techniques of subjection. The rehabilitation packages draw forth a repentant criminal, a grateful criminal, a self-loathing criminal, keen and anxious to complete the detailed work on the self that is required of them by a liberal order.

There is, arguably, a cynicism inherent in the rehabilitation packages: they give on the one hand—a connection to a child, a 'chance' to get back into the job market—but at the expense of those who do not meet the stringent eligibility requirement of, for example, the OxCAB assessment. Furthermore, it is clear that there still remains a necessity for anonymity to be retained with regard to members of the public using the Bureau. Although it is advertised that the branch acts in partnership with Springhill, the prisoner-advisers have never been identified as such to any clients. When asked to comment on anonymity and disclosure, the comments were varied

> *Oliver*: I think it's quite important, but not to the people who volunteer . . . they might not like prisoners giving them advice.
> *Liam*: I don't mind them knowing. They might look at it as . . . you're giving back and you're changing your life around.
> (Focus Group 2, 12 January 2012).

Although CAB staff recalled instances where the media were critical of the use of prisoners as advisers (with one referring to the 'Crooks Advice Bureau'), facilitators maintain that the prisoner status is of no more relevance to the job role than someone's age or sexuality. This is largely based on the quality of work that CAB has received from their prisoner-volunteers, the positive feedback, letters of thanks and even monetary contributions that members of the public have offered as a return for the service. Certainly, the invisible nature of the prisoner-adviser renders them able to exert their participation in ways which may not be afforded by their exposure in this environment. However, it could be argued that the elision of volunteers' identities as prisoners serves precisely to erase the 'prisoner' as 'citizen' while ensuring that he/she must simultaneously reproduce problematic civic regimes.

Performing *Less than Ideal* Citizenship

In addition to these critical perspectives, I would like to use the remainder of this paper to consider the ways in which prisoners perform informal activities that disrupt contemporary notions of good citizenship, including developing the notion of the prison as 'home' rather than a physical and emotional displacement from home.

There are many informal mechanisms that prisoners have developed to enable themselves to re-create a sense of 'normalcy' in their everyday prison lives via a belonging to broader networks and allegiances. A BBC documentary about life in the women's prison HMP Cornton Vale in Scotland, for example, describes how inmates Debbie and Gemma found that celebrity gossip magazines helped them to keep up-to-date with the goings on of the famous and glamorous—a world in which they were not likely to participate in a more corporeal sense if they were not incarcerated (BBC, 2008). There are also examples of attempts to retain the citizenship of other less-territorially-grounded communities, such as those of football supporters. An art teacher facilitating classes within prison noted that, although Steve hardly spoke, when he did, one very obvious thread of thinking permeated everything and this was Liverpool Football Club (Rudesind, 2006).

There are, of course, ways in which the 'civic death' of incarcerated offenders leads some to want to exert their citizenship rights in illicit ways. One prisoner blog explains his attempts to keep his non-taxable incomes to maintain his ability to provide for his family. He comments that, he is "desperately trying to keep a few projects going on on the outside, but people are just not responding quickly enough" (The Prisoner, 2006, 9 January). Their desire to re-assert the rights they have lost also extends to the many attempts to acquire contraband items, such as alcohol and mobile phones, resulting in vast commodity networks of supply and demand. Observational research within the prison environment by Valentine and Longstaff (1998) and Baer (2005) has also revealed that there is a desire for much more mundane, yet still contraband items such as herbs and spices, or toiletry items like perfume—those things that prisoners do not have regular access to on a daily basis and yet which command a sense of home and belonging therein.

For other prisoners, non-sanctioned activities constitute their only ability to access contact time with their family. Here, one can see how one inmate describes the activities of his cellmate at Parc Prison in Wales, UK

> His missus would turn up outside the prison every night with the kids to talk to him. She would park up on the pavement opposite the magistrates' court, facing our cell window. He would flick the light on and off three times. When she parked up he would know because she would toot her horn twice. They would shout to each other and tell each other about their day. He would ask her about how she was running his take-away and ask if there were any problems, and his son would should as loud as he could, "Abba, I love you!" (Arif, 2009, p. 57).

For many, they become accustomed and even welcomed into the community of the prison—a hidden world which Adrian Rudesind describes as 'Prisonland' (2006, p. 17). And, the same careful delineation of the rights and responsibilities of a British citizen can be applied to the unique, national identity of the 'prisoner'. Even within the prison itself, there are formal mechanisms which create the discourses of behaviour and punishment. Sara Ahmed describes this as the creation of prisons within prisons and bars within bars, where the punished 'prison citizen' will be forced to spend time in such things as the Segregation Unit—jail within prison. Thus inmates suffer the same social consequences of convicted citizens from the outside, such as being forced to leave their prison families, cellblocks, religious communities and jobs, to be placed under control within control and subjection to even greater episodes of discipline (Ahmed, 2008, p. 2).

Moreover, it can be argued that the right to participate is not automatically guaranteed by merely the serving of a sentence at Her Majesty's pleasure. In order to ascertain citizenship of Prisonland, inmates are expected to exert their responsibility as a convict by abiding to the new rules of prison. As Hayner and Ash illustrate

Even though he may wish, as an individual, to adhere rigidly to the rules and regulations of the administration, he must at the same time live up to the convict rule—'You must not squeal' (Hayner and Ash, 1939, p. 364).

There exists a whole host of informal ways in which an inmate can exert belonging to the prison community. This may be altering their use of language to adhere to prison jargon such as using references to 'screws' and 'grasses', 'going down the block' and 'doing bird'. Inmates may also become part of the structure of the prison wing, slotting into the hierarchy of the order, aligning themselves to particular gangs within the walls, or even altering their behaviour to deviate from conventional sex codes. They might become part of the system of supply and demand which is prominent in prison life, where everyday objects such as the foil in sweet wrappers become valuable trading commodities due to their alternative use as aids in drug-taking.

Ian Gunn, Governor of HMP Cornton Vale, intimates that the lives of prisoners are often so totally chaotic that

Prison becomes a haven in their chaotic lives ... Prison life gives [them] the security [they] didn't have in her childhood ... Some of these women believe this is the safest home they've ever had (Ian Gunn, BBC, 2008).

One prisoner, Gemma acknowledges: "What you see here. This is what I've got. This is my house". This 'inside' world soon becomes a way of life and, in many cases, a home—something that became clear to me even through the conversational language used when talking about the prison

JT: And so when you get *home*, oh sorry, I've said it again ...
Ian: [laughs]
Oliver: It's alright it is home.
Liam: I find myself saying that all the time ... when I'm on home leave, for instance D-cat prisoners can go home, I say to the missus or whatever, "I've got to go *home* [back to prison] tomorrow", I'm at home but I still say it.

(Focus Group 2, 12 January 2012).

Conclusion

To conclude this discussion, it is clear that, despite attempts to foster the notion of rehabilitation as geared towards the re-composition of the prisoner alongside contemporary imaginations of the ideal citizen, there are many reasons why prisoners will consistently achieve anything but that. In examining rehabilitation programmes developed to allow prisoners to exert their obligations and access the rights of the 'outside' world, this paper has illustrated how prisoners must perform as well as conform to these ideals with many genuinely desiring their own reform. Yet, despite all efforts to conform to the ideology of liberal society, the prisoner experiences a civic death during imprisonment. What is also apparent is that, once incarcerated, prisoners become intrinsically incorporated into and practise citizenship to the community of the prison, which is in many cases contra the manifesto of the 'outside' ideal. Furthermore, upon release offenders are still reminded of their status as 'prison citizens' and will inevitably be bound to this by their criminal record, prison experience and social stigma for the remainder of their lives. Thus, I want to suggest in closing that, despite their struggle to achieve the aspirations that the penal system drives them towards, prisoners paradoxically become part of an ideology which functions to posit still them as 'non-citizens'.

Notes

1. Her Majesty's Prison Service is a part of the Ministry of Justice department of the British government tasked with delivering public prison provision in England and Wales. Scotland and Northern Ireland have their own independent services (The Scottish Prison Service and the Northern Ireland Prison Service).
2. Pseudonyms have been used.

References

AHMED, S. (2008) The prison citizen, DifferenTakes, 54(Fall), pp. 1–4.
ARIF (2009) Inside times, in: PARC PRISONERS (Eds.) Inside Out: Real Life Stories from Behind Bars, pp. 56–65. Bedlinog: Accent Press.
BAER, L. D. (2005) Visual imprints on the prison landscape: a study on the decorations in prison cells, Tijdschrift voor Economische en Sociale Geografie, 96(2), pp. 209–217.
BAER, L. D. and RAVNEBERG, B. (2008) The outside and inside in Norwegian and English prisons, Geografiska Annaler, 90B(2), pp. 205–216.
BBC (2008) Girls behind bars. BBC Channel 1, 1 October.
BBC (2010) Our world—'Hard Labour'. BBC News, 10 January.
BBC (2012) Prisoner Martin Tate says he is not allowed to make calls in Welsh. BBC News South-West Wales (http://www.bbc.co.uk/news/uk-wales-south-west-wales-16679936; accessed 24 January 2012).
BEHAN, C. and O'DONNELL, I. (2008) Prisoners, politics and the polls, British Journal of Criminology, 48(3), pp. 319–336.
BLAIS, A., MASSICOTTE, L. and YOSHINAKA, A. (2001) Deciding who has the right to vote: a comparative analysis of election laws, Electoral Studies, 20(1), pp. 41–62.
BROWNLOW, A. (2011) Between rights and responsibilities: insurgent performance in an invisible landscape, Environment and Planning A, 43(6), pp. 1268–1286.
BURCHELL, G. (1996) Liberal government and techniques of the self, in: A. BARRY, T. OSBORNE and N. ROSE (Eds) Foucault and Political Reason: Liberalism, Neoliberalism and Rationalities of Government, pp. 19–36. London: University College London Press.
BURNETT, R. and MARUNA, S. (2006) The kindness of prisoners, Criminology and Criminal Justice, 6(1), pp. 83–106.
CHALLEEN, D. A. (1986) Making It Right: A Common Sense Approach to Criminal Justice. Aberdeen, SD: Melius and Peterson.
CHEAKALOS, C. (2004) New leash on life: in an innovative program, prison inmates find that raising puppies for the blind makes a difference, Smithsonian, 35(5), pp. 62–68.
CITIZENS ADVICE BUREAU (2012) About us. Citizens Advice Bureau (http://www.citizensadvice.org.uk/index/aboutus.htm; accessed 1 June 2012).
COMBESSIE, P. (2002) Marking the carceral boundary: penal stigma in the long shadow of the prison, Ethnography, 3(4), pp. 535–555.
CRUIKSHANK, B. (1999) The Will to Empower: Democratic Citizens and Other Subjects. Ithaca, NY: Cornell University Press.
DESFORGES, L., JONES, R. and WOODS, M. (2005) New geographies of citizenship, Citizenship Studies, 9(5), pp. 439–451.
DHAMI, M. K. (2005) Prisoner disenfranchisement policy: a threat to democracy?, Analyses of Social Issues and Public Policy, 5(1), pp. 235–247.

DIETRICH, S. (2002) Criminal records and employment: ex-offenders' thwarted attempts to earn a living for their families, in: A. E. HIRSCH, S. M. DIETRICH, R. LANDAU, P.D. SCHNEIDER *et al.* (Eds) *Every Door Closed: Barriers Facing Parents with Criminal Records*, pp. 13–26. Washington, DC: Center for Law and Social Policy and Philadelphia, PA: Community Legal Services, Inc.

ESMÉE FAIRBAIRN FOUNDATION (2004) *Rethinking crime and punishment: the report.* Esmée Fairbairn Foundation (http://www.rethinking.org.uk/informed/pdf/RCP%20The%20Report.pdf; accessed 7 February 2012).

EWALD, A. C. (2002) 'Civil death': the ideological paradox of criminal disenfranchisement law in the United States, *Wisconsin Law Review*, 2002(5), pp. 1045–1137.

FYFE, N. and MILLIGAN, C. (2003a) Out of the shadows: exploring contemporary geographies of the welfare voluntary sector, *Progress in Human Geography*, 27(4), pp. 397–413.

FYFE, N. and MILLIGAN, C. (2003b) Space, citizenship and the 'shadow state': exploring the voluntary welfare sector in Glasgow, *Environment and Planning A*, 35(11), pp. 2069–2086.

GAHIR, M., O'ROURKE, S., MONTEIRO, M. and REED, R. (2011) The unmet needs of deaf prisoners: a survey of prisons in England and Wales, *International Journal on Mental Health and Deafness*, 1(1) (http://www.ijmhd.org/index.php/ijmhd/article/view/4; accessed 1 February 2012).

GILMORE, R. W. (2007) *Golden Gulag: Prisons, Surpluses, Crisis, and Opposition in Globalizing California.* London: University of California Press.

HARMAN, J. J., SMITH, V. E. and EGAN, L. C. (2007) The impact of incarceration on intimate relationships, *Criminal Justice and Behavior*, 34(6), pp. 794–815.

HAYNER, N. S. and ASH, E. (1939) The prisoner community as a social group, *American Sociological Review*, 4(3), pp. 362–369.

HILL, L. and KOCH, C. (2011) The voting rights of incarcerated Australian citizens, *Australian Journal of Political Science*, 46(2), pp. 213–228.

ISIN, E. and NIELSEN, G. (2008) Introduction, in: E. ISIN and G. NIELSEN (Eds) *Acts of Citizenship*, pp. 1–12. London: Zed Books.

ITKOWITZ, H. and OLDAK, L. (1973) Restoring the ex-offender's right to vote: background and developments, *American Criminal Law Review*, 11, pp. 721–770.

ITV (2011) *Babies behind bars.* ITV Channel 1, 27 June.

JESSOP, B. (1988) Conservative regimes and the transition to post-Fordism: the cases of Britain and West Germany, in: M. GOTTDIENER and N. KOMNINOS (Eds) *Capitalist Development and Crisis Theory: Accumulation, Regulation and Spatial Restructuring.* London: Macmillan.

KAINOS COMMUNITY (2012) *Challenge to change.* Kainos Community (http://www.wix.com/kainoscommunity/kainoscommunity; accessed 1 June 2012).

KEYSSAR, A. (2000) *The Right to Vote: A Contested History of Democracy in the United States.* New York: Basic Books.

LEPOFSKY, J. and FRASER, J. C. (2003) Building community citizens: claiming the right to place-making in the city, *Urban Studies*, 40(1), pp. 127–142.

LOYD, J., BURRIDGE, A. and MITCHELSON, M. (2009) Thinking (and moving) beyond walls and cages: bridging immigrant justice and anti-prison organizing in the United States, *Social Justice*, 36(2), pp. 85–103.

MARTIN, L. L. and MITCHELSON, M. L. (2009) Geographies of detention and imprisonment: interrogating spatial practices of confinement, discipline, law, and state power, *Geography Compass*, 3(1), pp. 459–477.

MAY, D. C. and WOOD, P. B. (2005) What influences offenders' willingness to serve alternative sanctions?, *The Prison Journal*, 85(2), pp. 145–167.

McCAY, V. (2010) The horror of being deaf and in prison, *American Annals of the Deaf*, 155(3), pp. 311–321.

METCALF, M., ANDERSON, T. and ROLFE, H. (2001) *Barriers to employment for offenders and ex-offenders. Part one: barriers to employment for offenders and ex-offenders.* Research Report No. 155, Department for Work and Pensions.

MILLER, K. R. (2004) Linguistic diversity in a deaf prison population: implications for due process, *Journal of Deaf Studies and Deaf Education*, 9(1), pp. 112–119.

MINISTRY OF JUSTICE (2011) *HMP offender statistics 2010/11 Annex C: statistics on offenders.* Ministry of Justice, London.

MINISTRY OF JUSTICE (2012) *Offender behaviour programmes (OBPs).* Ministry of Justice, London (http://www.justice.gov.uk/offenders/before-after-release/obp; accessed 1 June 2012).

NOMS (NATIONAL OFFENDER MANAGEMENT SERVICE) (2011) *National offender management service annual report 2010/11: management information addendum.* Ministry of Justice, London.

ODPM (Office of the Deputy Prime Minister) (2002) *Reducing re-offending of ex-prisoners.* Report by the Social Inclusion Unit, ODPM, London.

PAIN, R. (2009) Globalized fear? Towards an emotional geopolitics, *Progress in Human Geography*, 33(4), pp. 466–486.

PALLOT, J. (2005) Russia's penal peripheries: space, place and penalty in Soviet and post-Soviet Russia, *Transactions of the Institute of British Geographers*, 30(1), pp. 98–112.

PATRICK, R. (n.d.) *Prisoner voting and active citizenship*. The Youth Foundation (http://www.youngfoundation.org/blog/policy/prisoner-voting-and-active-citizenship; accessed 1 February 2012).

THE PRISONER (2006) *The prisoner: a life in the day of a British prisoner* (http://theprisonersdiary.blogspot.com; accessed 7 February 2012).

ROSE, N. (1996) Governing 'advanced' liberal democracies, in: A. BARRY, T. OSBORNE and N. ROSE (Eds) *Foucault and Political Reason: Liberalism, Neoliberalism and Rationalities of Government*, pp. 37–64. London: University College London Press.

ROSE, N. (2000) Government and control, *British Journal of Criminology*, 40, pp. 321–339.

ROTTINGHAUS, B. and BALDWIN, G. (2007) Voting behind bars: explaining variation in international enfranchisement practices, *Electoral Studies*, 26(3), pp. 688–698.

RUDESIND, A. (2006) *Bang Up for Men: The Smell of Prison*. London: Starborn Books.

SLAPPER, G. (2011) Opinion: the ballot box and the jail cell, *The Journal of Criminal Law*, 75, pp. 1–3.

SMITH, M. P. and GUARNIZO, L. E. (2009) Global mobility, shifting borders and urban citizenship, *Tijdschrift voor Economische en Sociale Geografie*, 100(5), pp. 610–622.

SMITH, S. J. (1989) Society, space and citizenship: a human geography for the 'new times', *Transactions of the Institute of British Geographers*, 14(2), pp. 144–156.

STORYBOOK DADS (2012) *StoryBook dads home* (http://www.storybookdads.co.uk; accessed 31 May 2012).

THOMPSON, J. (2000) Critical citizenship: Boal, Brazil and theatre in prisons, *Annual Review of Critical Psychology*, 2, pp. 181–191.

TOCH, H. (2000) Altruistic activity as correctional treatment, *International Journal of Offender Therapy and Comparative Criminology*, 44(3), pp. 270–278.

UGGEN, C., MANZA, J. and BEHRENS, A. (2004) Less than the average citizen: stigma, role transition, and the civic reintegration of convicted felons, in: S. MARUNA and R. IMMARIGEON (Eds) *After Crime and Punishment: Pathways to Offender Reintegration*, pp. 261–293. Cullompton: Willan Publishing.

UGGEN, C., MANZA, J. and THOMPSON, M. (2006) Citizenship, democracy, and the civic reintegration of criminal offenders, *Annals of the American Academy of Political and Social Science*, 605, pp. 281–310.

UNLOCK (2004) *Barred from voting: the right to vote for sentenced prisoners*. UNLOCK: The National Association of Ex-Offenders (http://www.unlock.org.uk/userfiles/file/Votes/Barred%20from%20Voting%20Campaign%20Briefing%20Paper%20%282004%29.pdf; accessed 1 February 2012).

VALENTINE, G. and LONGSTAFF, B. (1998) Doing porridge: food and social relations in a male prison, *Journal of Material Culture*, 3(2), pp. 131–152.

VERGARA, C. J. (1995) *The New American Ghetto*. New Brunswick, NJ: Rutgers University Press.

WACQUANT, L. (2000) The new 'peculiar institution': on the prison as surrogate ghetto, *Theoretical Criminology*, 4(3), pp. 377–389.

WACQUANT, L. (2001) Deadly symbiosis: when ghetto and prison meet and mesh, in: D. GARLAND (Eds) *Mass Imprisonment in the United States*, pp. 82–120. London: Sage.

WACQUANT, L. (2009) The body, the ghetto and the penal state, *Qualitative Sociology*, 32(1), pp. 101–129.

Negotiating Absence and Presence: Rural Muslims and 'Subterranean' Sacred Spaces

RHYS DAFYDD JONES

Abstract. Rural Muslims' lives have received less attention than those of their urban counterparts in secular liberal democracies. Muslims' experiences of rural regions are characterised by a visible absence on the one hand, but a physical presence on the other. In this paper, the concept of the subterranean is invoked to understand the negotiation between superficial absences and physical presence. Conscious of the clandestine associations of the subterranean, it is argued that this illustrates a tactical making-do with limited resources rather than self-segregation. It is concluded that absences and presence in rural multiculturalism are complex, contingent and have a temporal nature.

Introduction

The past 20 years have seen a proliferation of work relating to the experiences of Muslims living in liberal secular democracies. Such studies have been brought about, in part, as a result of the geopolitical context in which Muslims in Europe, North America and elsewhere are vilified as intolerant, illiberal and a threat to security (Werbner, 2000; Modood, 2006). These studies have an overwhelmingly urban focus: regional centres or national capital cities such as Sydney (Dunn, 2004), Edinburgh (Hopkins, 2006) and London (Eade, 1996) provide staple case studies. This is not surprising: the city has long been considered as a vibrant and dynamic arena in which different groups come together (Amin, 2002) and Muslims in the UK have an overwhelmingly urban profile (Peach, 2006; Brice, 2009). However, the experiences of Muslims outside these metropolitan settings, particularly in rural areas, have so far been overlooked. Examining these more marginalised regions is worthy as the everyday lives of Muslims in rural areas are often characterised by encountering and negotiating absences. Unlike urban centres, which have sizeable Muslim populations and long histories of the establishment of services and sacred spaces (Naylor and Ryan, 2002, 2003), rural areas are often characterised by small populations with a fairly recent history of settlement and, as a result, a dependence on makeshift and contingent sacred spaces and religious services. Where there are campaigns to establish purpose-built facilities, they are often opposed on grounds of incompatibility with 'rural' lifestyles (Bugg, 2012). As a result, Muslims and other religious minorities in rural areas are often less visible: there are fewer people wearing religious dress to be found and their sacred spaces, where they exist, are invariably 'storefront' mosques (Slymovics, 1996). Consequently, rural Muslims experience a relatively visible absence from the landscape and typically have fewer religious services than their urban counterparts.

Adopting the rhetoric of the hidden in studying particular groups in rural areas is not limited to Muslims. Studies of marginalised and vulnerable categories of people in rural areas have often invoked the language of absence in their studies, highlighting 'concealed', 'silent' and 'hidden' characteristics. Milbourne and Cloke (2006, p. 2), for example, note that "rural homelessness remains 'invisible' in the rural landscape; concealed within the physical socio-cultural and political fabric of rural space". Such rhetoric is also applied to studies of people from Black and Minority Ethnic (BME) backgrounds in rural areas (Neal, 2002; Robinson, 2003; Robinson and Gardner, 2004), which provide useful studies of the experiences of being simultaneously visible (such as the target for racial abuse) and invisible (from policy priorities). Alongside these hidden experiences, there also exists a discursive absence in which particular groups are excluded from popular imaginations of an idyllised rural space. As Gruffudd (1994, 1995) and Neal (2002) have remarked, political élites often evoke a homogeneous rural idyll as a synecdoche for the nation, which emphasises Christian, White and 'straight' characteristics; alternative subjectivities are absent from such representations. More banal forms of geographical imaginations, such as television dramas, also exclude bodies that do not conform to this idyll. In 2011, the producer of the British detective programme, *Midsomer Murders*, courted controversy by defending the lack of BME actors in the programme by suggesting that it reflected 'the realism' of rural English society, reifying these discursive absences, overlooking evidence of a longstanding BME presence in rural areas (Bressey, 2009). Like these groups, Muslims are also absent from the popular imaginations of rural spaces, while Islamic services are hard to identify in rural areas (Dafydd Jones, 2010). Consequently, Muslims in rural areas encounter not only a visible absence, but also a discursive absence in which they are written out of rural space.

However, characterising the quotidian experiences of Muslims in rural regions as purely absent and marginalised is problematic for two reasons. First, there is a danger of constructing local Muslims as passive actors, suggesting that only global events shaped by the *zeitgeist* of the 'War on Terror' on an abstract global scale influence their lives, rather than events or processes that are more localised (Pain and Smith, 2008). Such a construction overlooks a myriad of actions that arise from Muslims' own agency and action they take to establish services and facilities in the region and act as citizens. Secondly, such an approach constructs Muslims as docile populations who are written-out of rural space and perpetually victimised. Other emotive experiences, then, such as happiness, boredom, indifference and contentment, need to be recognised, rather than left unacknowledged. This paper suggests that Muslims' absences from rural areas are only superficial and are largely based on small populations and a visible absence. As with rural BME populations, Muslims' presence can be seen "beneath the surface of the rural landscape" (Bressey, 2009, p. 387). Despite a lack of purpose-built and visible facilities, Muslims in rural areas make use of a variety of everyday spaces and sites to perform their religious identities. These sites and spaces, which are often appropriated and diverted into sacred spaces, serve as bases for small but vibrant networks of local Muslims. In this paper, I invoke the concept of the subterranean to discuss the dual experiences of Muslims' visible absence and physical presence in rural areas. This concept is particularly pertinent in acknowledging the different ways of being absent and present that are experienced in rural Muslims' everyday lives. While the subterranean is often attributed with sinister and clandestine overtones, I argue that it also acknowledges the tactical making-do of resources available that characterises rural minority religious groups. Consequently, it provides an understanding of rural Muslims as active citizens developing services for their own needs rather than as marginalised and absent from rural areas.

The paper is structured as follows: the first section outlines recent conceptualisations of the subterranean and notes its key features. The second section introduces the case study of Muslims in west Wales. In the third section, I examine the ways in which the region's Muslims encounter and negotiate absence and presence, examining the significance of particular makeshift and contingent sacred spaces which allow for the formation of networks of religious capital. I then move to discuss the implications of this visible absence from the rural landscape for local Muslim organisations in the fourth section. In the fifth section, I acknowledge the potential danger of evoking a subterranean metaphor to understand the experiences of Muslims in west Wales and I outline the way that subterranean sites resonate more with understanding Muslims in the region as pioneers rather than a self-segregating community. The final section offers some tentative conclusions.

Subterranean Spaces

Much attention in recent years has been given towards the subterranean, both as *actual* spaces beneath the ground and as *virtual* spaces, largely referred to as the 'underground'. Accounts of these spatial imaginations discuss such diverse aspects as colonialism (Scott, 2008), Victorian imagination (Williams, 2008), infrastructure (Pike, 2005), urban exploration (Garrett, 2011), and popular music (Solomon, 2005). In these works, two characteristics emerge which are central to the subterranean: invisibility and verticality.

Invisibility is a key feature of the subterranean. The distinction between the surface and the sub-surface is based largely on what can and cannot be seen. In an occularcentric society, acts, processes and spaces beneath the ground are constructed as absent as they cannot be seen. Yet, as Bishop (2011, p. 272) notes, such engagement with the surface always assumes a latent depth to it. Subterranean spaces, then, are out of *sight*, but not necessarily out of *site*. Many services and infrastructures that sustain contemporary societies exist in a subterranean state. Sewage systems, electricity cables and even spare costumes at Disney World are separated from the surface so as to preserve its aesthetic appearance (Pike, 2005); the successful and smooth operation of the surface depends on their functionality. Consequently, there is a distinction between form and function (Cresswell, 1996) that underpins the division between surface and sub-surface. However, other techniques and media, such as sonar (Bishop, 2011) disrupt this distinction and facilitate the discovery, surveillance and mapping of the subterranean world in the same way that visual technologies have enabled mapping the earth's surface. Alongside invisibility, these studies document a desire to make the invisible visible and to uncover knowledge. Venturing into the subterranean realm is a well-covered theme both in literature (Williams, 2008) and in academia (Garrett, 2011), which appropriates such verbs as 'digging', 'excavating' and 'exposing' in the search for knowledge. Beck (2011), however, calls for more work on understanding the nature of absence in itself and, in response, I examine how 'invisible' spaces are lived religious landscapes (Kong, 2005) in the everyday lives of Muslims in west Wales, negotiating absence and presence.

Studies of the subterranean also evoke a vertical ontology. Such ontology is central not only in distinguishing between what is seen and what is not seen, but also in gaining knowledge. Scott (2008), for example, discusses how colonisers' anxieties of the subterranean Peruvian mines led to their incorporation in mapping projects. For Perkins and Dodge (2009), satellite images are akin to an all-seeing eye that succeeds in mapping the earth's surface, capturing its secrets and allowing for recording movements and resources. Thus, verticality brings with it an empowered god-like position that detaches the viewer from a position of the viewed, privileging the researcher. Yet, a strict vertical ontology need not be a requirement for the subterranean. Its use is in distinguishing between what is seen (down towards the surface) and what is not (from the surface downwards); there are other ways of becoming invisible. Williams (2008, pp. 18–19) acknowledges the role of the horizontal dimension found in 19th-century American literature in contrast to the verticality found in European literature. Twentieth-century British authors such as C. S. Lewis and J. K. Rowling have also created subterranean worlds on a horizontal axis: Narnia is initially entered through a wardrobe and Diagon Alley through a tavern. The vertical element is missing in figurative conceptions of the underground, as Solomon's (2005) case study of hip-hop in Istanbul demonstrates. Arguably, it is this vertical ontology that separates the subterranean as an actual space from the underground as a virtual space.

Alongside these two characteristics, there are three recurring themes in discussions of the social underground. First, the underground is seen as a refuge and subsequently as a space for secrets. To some extent, this ties in with issues of visibility, as the surface cannot be penetrated by the ordinary gaze. As Casanova (2005) notes, marginalised religious would hold secret meetings to avoid persecution during the 17th century; some wealthy Catholics in England would incorporate 'priest-holes' into their houses so that they could continue their dissimulationist Catholicism. Secondly, it is a space of resistance and threat. The use of the word underground to denote resistance groups in Nazi-occupied Europe conveys this sense, as well as talk about criminalised activities being 'driven underground', where they cannot be regulated. As Scott (2008) notes, the subterranean was a source of anxiety for 16th-century Spanish colonisers in Peru as it was a space where indigenous beliefs could continue despite evangelising processes. This leads to the final theme, the underground as counter-cultural. Such spaces are seen as a haven for difference and, subsequently, a threat to the maintained order. Solomon (2005), for example, discusses how the Internet and select clubs allowed Turkish hip-hop artists to disseminate their music while avoiding the censorship that would come with conventional routes of production, which would have objected to the content and language of the songs, evoking the underground as a sentiment and process rather than a physical space. While these three themes feature heavily in the literature, other themes identified through a close reading of Williams's *Notes on the Underground* (2008) are absent. Most notably, Williams highlights the underground as containing spaces of richness to be tapped by humankind, the central theme to Verne's *Les Indes noires*.

Alongside this, the underground as frontier is another common theme in many works, where pioneers make tactical use of the resources they find in subterranean worlds. This paper attempts to broaden understandings of the underground by examining these latter two themes rather than resorting to clandestine caricatures.

Case Study Overview: Muslims in West Wales

According to the 2001 census[1] there were 750 Muslims (or 0.2 per cent of the region's population) to be found in west Wales, comprising the Unitary Authorities of Carmarthenshire, Ceredigion and Pembrokeshire. Twenty-eight Muslims living and working in rural west Wales were interviewed between September 2008 and October 2009 for doctoral fieldwork. Participants came from a range of ages and ethnic, national and vocational backgrounds, with different life-courses and different levels of religiosity. Unlike the respondents, the researcher is an atheist with a loose and liberal Congregationalist background; like some of the respondents, he was born, lives and works in the region and speaks Welsh. These different insider/outsider dynamics were negotiated throughout the research process.

Muslims in the region of study—which largely excluded the post-industrial south-east of Carmarthenshire, spanning from Ammanford to Llanelli—tended to live in and around five market towns in the region: Aberystwyth, Cardigan, Carmarthen, Lampeter and Haverfordwest, all of which have fewer than 20 000 inhabitants. There is no evidence of residential clustering at a more local scale, suggesting that Muslims are dispersed within these settlements, although in some proximity to each other. The services found in these towns align with the industrial niches occupied by Muslims in the region; many worked in one of three hospitals in the vicinity, or studied at one of its two universities,[2] one of which has a Centre for the Study of Islam.

Of the 28 Muslims interviewed, only three had lived in the region for more than 10 years. This suggests both a fairly recent history of settlement in the region and a high level of turnover of Muslim residents.[3] While there are records of Malaysian students studying at Aberystwyth since 1946, many of whom were Muslims, and anecdotal evidence of Muslim doctors in Lampeter for a brief period in the 1960s, it appears that it is only towards the 1980s that sustained Muslim settlement came to the region. This can be attributed in part to the increase in recruitment of international students following a change in government policy in 1980 which allowed universities to charge differential fees, leading to the development of international recruitment as a strategy of expansion. However, as many Muslims in the region study at local universities—including at Lampeter's Centre for the Study of Islam—or work in local hospitals in more junior positions, there is a steady and quick turnover; many appear to stay for three of four years before moving to more urban areas with perceived better career opportunities. Hospitals and universities are important nodes for local Islamic networks as Muslims in west Wales are drawn from diverse cultural backgrounds and local worship facilities are often arranged around these sites rather than based on ethno-national identities. While Peach (2006, p. 357) notes that, as one travels north in England, "the Muslim population becomes progressively more South Asian in general and Pakistani in particular", those in west Wales come from a range of ethnic and national backgrounds. As constructions of British Muslims are often racialised and based on a southern Asian ethnicity, Muslims with other backgrounds often constitute a 'hidden minority' that is absent from British integration discourses (Nagel and Staeheli, 2008) as well as lay imaginations of British Muslims.

Both the turnover of Muslim residents and the distances between settlements have created challenges for organisations such as the West Wales Islamic Cultural Association (WWICA), which seeks to develop services for the region's Muslims. First, the small population means that service provision is dependent on one or two people with relevant expertise; should they leave, there is a need to try and find a suitable replacement to continue such services as Qur'an or Arabic classes. Furthermore, newcomers to the region often spoke of initial difficulties in finding and accessing Islamic services, further jeopardising continuity. Secondly, the distances between the five main towns, underpinned by a comparatively weak public transport system that is characteristic of rural areas in the UK (Gray *et al.*, 2001), means that services are often localised and limited. There are, however, some attempts to organise more specialist services on a regional basis (such as the aforementioned classes), which succeed in attracting some worshippers from other areas in the region. However, the limited range of services available in the region (such as a lack of particular *halal* foods) meant that many participants would travel to cities outside the region, such as Swansea, where a wider range of services could be accessed, 'leapfrogging' the more regional provision. As a consequence, the Muslim population in west Wales is fairly fragmented among more localised networks, with ensuring the continuity of particular services gaining precedence over more strategic developments. As I discuss in the next section, local Muslims depend on makeshift and contingent sacred spaces that occupy subterranean spaces, perpetuating their relative invisibility.

Negotiating Absence and Presence: 'Subterranean' Sacred Spaces

Muslims in west Wales occupy a position in which they are simultaneously absent and present: they are visibly absent, on the one hand, but physically present on the other. One way in which this juxtaposition is experienced is through the region's Islamic sacred spaces. These spaces are invariably 'storefront' mosques (Slymovics, 1996): often housed in such everyday spaces as former gymnasia, church halls, or above restaurants, the façades of these buildings used as sacred spaces do not attest to the presence of the acts of worship that take place within. While Muslims in cities would also worship in such storefront spaces (Eade, 1996; Slymovics, 1996), the uses of these sacred spaces are in many ways more absent in rural areas, as they are typically not owned or under the full control of local Muslims or Islamic organisations. These 'storefront' mosques and prayer-rooms can be classified into two categories: makeshift and contingent sacred spaces. The former are spaces that are momentarily made sacred through ritual—such as empty classrooms being used for prayer—before being returned to the secular and/or profane *status quo*. The latter are spaces that are diverted from their original use to function as sacred spaces; the aesthetics may reflect the original condition of the building, which may or may not be modified over time to facilitate Islamic worship. In some cases, such as the Old Gymnasium mosque in Aberystwyth, local Muslims do not own the premises and adaptations are often negotiated, dependent on the University and slow to develop. These sacred spaces which are used by many of the region's Muslims in their everyday lives are subterranean spaces: there is an absence from the superficial level—the streetscape—countered with a presence beneath the surface.

In the first instance, these storefront sacred spaces are sites in which believers of a shared faith can come together. To a large extent, they serve as 'convergence spaces' (Routledge, 2003) for local Muslims, dispersed throughout the locality, to come together in a single place, helping to foster a sense of identity. Such sites facilitate the simultaneous bonding and bridging accumulation of social capital (Putnam, 2000, pp. 68–69): they allow bonding in the sense that they bring local Muslims together, but also through bridging ethnic, national, age and other differences. Alongside the processes of social capital that are accumulated by such spaces are processes of religious capital. Religious capital is simultaneously a productive process (through praying, giving to charity, etc.) and a product of religious activity (in providing instructions for living, etc.—see Iannaccone, 1990); it is "a resource that individuals and faith groups can access for their own personal well-being, but also 'donate' as a gift to the wider community" (Baker and Skinner, 2006, p. 11), drawing on shared faith and beliefs to invest in particular structures. It is unsurprising then that, as a result of these practices, explicitly religious acts—particularly those concerned with devotion—are central to the function and development of such spaces. Prayer is regarded as the second most important tenant of Islam (after the declaration of faith) and finding a place suitable for prayer was the prime motivator for the development of these sites.

However, the use of these sacred spaces—even those used exclusively by local Muslims—is not limited to devotional rites; they are also used for a range of more temporal activities such as women's groups and language classes. Similarly, local Muslim restauranteurs would take it in turn to cook for students using the Old Gymnasium mosque in Aberystwyth during fast-breaking. As well as bonding through sharing food in a ritualised breaking of fast, such actions also allow for hospitality and pastoral care to be extended to young people at significant stages in their life-courses: leaving home for university. As with other temporal services (Beaumont, 2008a, 2008b), religious capital is important in realising these provisions, both through accessing the resources that are hand and in the motivation for such deeds (Iannacone, 1990). Consequently, these sacred spaces serve as arenas where more than devotional rites and religious instruction take place; they seek to become more rounded 'community centres' that offer a range of activities for local believers. As Ley (2008) argues in his analysis of similar provision by churches in Vancouver, faith-based organisation often fill gaps following cuts to public services, as well as accommodating particular cultural needs.

These sacred spaces are also important sites that help to formulate a sense of community among local Muslims. They allow Muslims to come together in an area where they are largely dispersed. These sites can also act as an arena for newcomers to get to know other Muslims in the region. For some respondents, meeting other Muslims in the vicinity was useful as it allowed people with similar values and religious identities to come together. Fatima, an international student at a local university, mentioned that she felt excluded from many of her non-Muslim peers, as most student events would revolve around alcohol

> When I was looking for universities I would go into the website of the universities and check if they had a Muslim students' society. My socialising is not the same as other people. In the beginning it was very important for me to have Muslim Society, and see if they arranged events very

often; when I got here I got to know that there isn't one; there was before. When you're alone, it helps to talk with other Muslim people who share the same spirituality as you and the practice level are approximately the same.

While Muslim students consider universities as liberal sites of tolerance, they are also places which can promote exclusion due to the nature of student events and practices (Hopkins, 2011). This echoes comments by Brice (2009, p. 231) that Muslims "living in less segregated areas actually tended to strengthen religious identity and by definition weaken cultural integration". Consequently, many of the region's Muslims welcome opportunities to go to events where alcohol is not served; sacred spaces allow access to such events, such as those organised by Islamic students' societies.

Meeting other Muslims also normalises the experiences of being Muslim in the region. This can combat feelings of isolation among Muslim children, as one parent mentioned

> *Saeeda*: Until my kids got involved with it [Qur'an classes], the only other Muslim people that they knew were their distant relatives in [English cities]. They wouldn't interact with Muslim people except for my husband's friends from work; they're the only Muslim people that they met. They didn't have any Muslim peers, so it was difficult, it's difficult to grow up being Muslim in a rural community; I think that's more profound then, as an adult, the isolation more profound because it's more meaningful when you're small, I think.

Muslim children in the region—particularly those attending primary schools and living in smaller settlements—would often be the 'only Muslim in the school'. Saeeda states that her children feel isolated because they did not have much opportunity to meet other Muslim children in the region, and are marked out as different which could lead to bullying. The Qur'an and Arabic classes organised by WWICA in Carmarthen were useful for allowing Muslim children to come together, normalising the experience of being a Muslim child in rural Wales, and helping to combat isolation. To an extent, then, this can be considered a peer-based network that allows informal support for Muslim children.

However, it is not only children who would place value on accessing these spaces and celebrating their Muslim identities. A large majority of respondents, even those with more secular and irreligious outlooks, placed value on knowing that they could attend the mosque on particular occasions

> *Noor*: I have my own community and I like to socialise with other people as well, so I don't like to be stuck in a small community, especially when it doesn't affect my religious views or whatever, I can do it at home ... So, I have Muslim friends and I have non-Muslim friends as well. It's nice to have Muslim friends that you can share things with, like when you break fast in Ramadan, we get together and we have dinner together etc., it's nice to share such things.

Noor, an international student, wanted to meet other Muslims and practise her religion while in the region, but did not want to do spend her time only among other Muslims. This suggests that Muslims of varying levels of religiosity use these sacred spaces, but do so in a manner that fits in with their lifestyles. Tactical use is made by Muslims of these sacred spaces as an opportunity to meet other Muslims in the region, supporting the position taken by Phillips (2006) in her critique of criticisms of British multiculturalism having apparently encouraged a segregated society (Cantle, 2004).

The use of these sacred sites as convergence spaces for Muslims in west Wales raises interesting questions about publicity and privacy. The nature of the acts that take place within these spaces is public: communal worship, interaction and networking. However, the spaces that host these acts are unmistakably private, owned by private citizens or non-Muslim organisations such as local universities. Such a relationship between privacy and publicity is not unconventional: Staeheli (1996), for example, has expressed how women's action groups problematise the public/private division, and other arenas in which public acts take place are private spaces, such as shopping centres (Staeheli and Mitchell, 2008). However, unlike shopping centres, mosques serve as convergence spaces and sites for over-spill activities, whereas activities at shopping centres are focused on the individual and are more tightly regulated. Such a relationship between public acts and private spaces is characteristic of what Fraser (1990) terms a 'subaltern counter-public', an arena in which particular interests judged beyond the scope of the public can be addressed and gradually made more 'mainstream'. As a consequence, using such private settings for public purposes suggests a making-do with the facilities available: Staeheli (1996) notes how the public activities of women's campaign groups rested on the private space of the home to co-ordinate these tactics.

Implications of Absence

The storefront nature of these mosques in west Wales, however, can create difficulties in bringing Muslims together. Their subterranean ontology can create difficulties for some Muslims—particularly newcomers to the area—in accessing the sacred space and the subsequent activities and services. Barack, another student, details how he only learned of the Old Gymnasium mosque in Aberystwyth through chance

> When I moved into my accommodation, I found myself having a Jordanian PhD student as my warden who was in my flat, and he had been here for a good three or four years and was a Muslim, and he told me a bit about the mosque, and he told me about where to find *halal* chicken etc.; he sort of introduced me to many other stuff around town.

It was only through chance that his hall warden was a Muslim that introduced Barack to the facility and the possibility of meeting other Muslims or partaking in Islamic rituals and events. Other Muslim newcomers also reported initial difficulties in finding and accessing services available. Even after local Muslims had accessed services in their own localities, they appeared unaware of what was available in nearby settlements. Ali, a member of WWICA's committee, mentions how a Muslim from Haverfordwest would pass Carmarthen to send his son to Islamic classes in Swansea, a city twice the distance away

> There was a gentleman from Haverfordwest, and he didn't know that there was a kind of school on Sunday for children, and he had his own private arrangement, he was planning to drive to Swansea every week

and for his children to go to Swansea's Islamic school, then he found out about the one here. I still feel that for others, probably nobody knows that there is a group of Muslims who are working here and running a kind of Sunday school. Once somebody finds out, they get surprised, 'Oh, it's been running for the last seven, eight years, and I didn't know!'

Such an occurrence is unsurprising considering the reliance WWICA had on makeshift sacred spaces. It would hire church halls for these classes and other functions when they were needed. While meeting immediate devotional needs, these spaces could not serve as a base (enabling more spin-off activities to develop) and perpetuated Muslims' invisibility in the region. A consequence of the visual absence of these subterranean sacred spaces is that Muslims in the vicinity who would like to access and possibly become involved in helping to organise these services may not be able to do so. This poses a particular challenge in a situation where there is a quick and steady turnover of Muslims. An extended organisation could help to stabilise the delivery of some services, as well as allowing for more social capital to be accumulated and more connections to be made.

A second consequence of the visual absence and the limited awareness other Muslims may have of local Islamic services and organisations concerns the ability of such groups to represent west Wales' Muslims at large. As Sanghera and Thapar-Bjökert (2008) illustrate, there is a need for researchers to question the capacity of various organisations as speaking for Muslims beyond the organisation's members. Different views, traditions and priorities may exist among Muslims who are not actively involved with WWICA or other organisations, and these may remain absent from any counter-public arena. Consequently, the private space that subaltern counter-publics inhabit in order to organise themselves can inhibit their representational capacity if that privacy creates difficulties in access.

Pioneer Spaces

Adopting the vocabulary of the subterranean to understand the experiences of Muslims in west Wales and their sacred spaces is not without its shortcomings. The subterranean, which rests on the distinction between the surface and sub-surface levels, could inadvertently reify the discourse of segregationist British multiculturalism and British Muslims living 'parallel lives' that the Cantle report (2004, p. 9) and others have prompted; a discourse that Phillips (2006) and others have challenged. Furthermore, the rhetoric of the subterranean has clandestine overtones. The subterranean has been viewed as a space of threat at least since the 16th century (Scott, 2008) and there is a danger that adopting this subterranean concept reifies an association between British Muslims and these attributes. However, the argument I make in this paper is that the subterranean ontology is much broader than these themes and there is a need to think about it in more holistic terms, incorporating other themes that recur in Williams' (2008) study, such as the underground as a space of resource and mineral wealth. In this section, I highlight how the subterranean sacred spaces used by Muslims in west Wales are a consequence of the context of Muslims' settlement in west Wales, rather than a desire to conceal themselves.

The use of these subterranean sacred spaces represents a making-do with the resources available. Old gymnasia or the upstairs of Bangladeshi restaurants are used due to the connections with local stakeholders, both through social capital—such as local universities—and through religious capital—such as local Muslim businessmen—but also through other faith-based organisations, such as the Carmarthen's Catholic church. This making-do represents a tactic

> A calculated action determined by the absence of a proper locus ... The space of the tactic is the space of the other. Thus it must play on and with a terrain imposed on it and organized by the law of a foreign power (de Certeau, 1984, p. 37).

The tactic is an appropriate concept to understand the use of these everyday spaces as sacred spaces as it acknowledges the discrepancy between the religious and spiritual capital and the societal culture in the region which is secular, (small-c) christian[4] and with limited experience of multicultural encounters. It is against this backdrop that the region's Muslims develop their sacred spaces.

An appropriate foil to de Certeau's concept is Scott's (1985, 1990) anthropological work related to the perceived absence of peasant resistance (in the form of mass demonstrations, etc.) to the mechanisation of Malaysia's agricultural sector in the late 1970s. While de Certeau's rhetoric is dualistic and oppositional, Scott allows for more subtlety and nuances. Scott's work is highly appropriate for engaging with questions about absence and presence as his thesis revolves around a reading of the 'full transcript'—considering actions such as rumour, sabotage and *graffiti* that occur in more liminal spaces—that shows the myriad forms of resistance that can occur (Scott, 1985, p. 284). Consequently, his work allows for the conceptualisation of resistance as "not directly to overthrow or transform a system of domination but rather to survive—today, this week, this season—within it" (Scott, 1985, p. 301).

As the previous section has articulated, the subterranean sacred spaces experienced by Muslims in west Wales facilitate these Muslims' practice of their religious identities within a context that does not dominate them, but in which such practices are difficult to fulfil. The tactical use of these available spaces rests on five factors.

First, the small population means that there is often insufficient demand to establish and maintain sacred spaces. Not only is there no 'critical mass' that would give a threshold, say, to justify buying and remodelling a permanent home for a mosque, but the dispersal of the region's Muslims to various towns that are some distance away means that focus on development is often localised. Furthermore, balancing work and educational commitments with religious duties means that the local is the appropriate scale for organisation. It would often be impractical to travel 40 minutes to attend the communal *jumm'ah* prayer on Fridays, but not to obtain *halal* foodstuffs or Arabic lessons for children. However, it is the former which serves as the catalyst for the development of sacred spaces.

Secondly, and as a consequence of the first factor, Muslims in west Wales have less political capital than their counterparts in other, more urban, areas, as Kamal notes

> What my perception is [it] all boils down to numbers. If you're not that many in numbers, [in a] democracy it's difficult to make your voice heard; the council would be interested in you and your problems, MPs will also, you know, come and listen to you.

While there has been some descriptive representation among local councils in the past,[5] a lack of concentration of Muslim residents in any particular ward even within the region's towns, means that there is little political capital to be made by attempting to court the Muslim vote. This lack of political capital brings about a reliance on active citizenship and utilising connections with other local stakeholders, such as universities and hospitals.

Thirdly, Muslims in west Wales benefit from transnational flows, but not to the same extent as those in London. Eade (1996), for example, highlights the role taken by the Bangladeshi High Commission in the establishment of the East London Mosque, demonstrating the influence of the politics of propinquity (Amin, 2004) and the 'thickness' of transnational connections. While it is true that the development of the Old Gymnasium at Aberystwyth came from the desire to attract international students to the university and that the Centre for the Study of Islam in Lampeter was part-funded by money from Gulf states, these did not bring about a development in more extensive—and more visible—services, but those which met the basic needs of the local Muslim populace. Transnational flows are important, but are limited in what they bring.

Fourthly, Muslims in west Wales appear to have a fairly recent history of settlement in the region. Compared with areas such as London, Liverpool or Cardiff, with their significant Muslim populations and long-established places of worship (Naylor and Ryan, 2002, 2003; Gilliat-Ray and Mellor, 2010), there is a limited foundation for the next generation to build on. Muslims worshippers in west Wales are still in the process of building capacity through using makeshift and contingent sacred spaces which they are yet to out-grow. The fact that they benefit in many ways from provision via local stakeholders may also lessen pressures to buy and develop their own sites. Fifthly, and relatedly, the quick and steady turnover of Muslim residents in the region means that demand for particular services cannot be predicted and may heighten a dependency on stakeholders. The peripheral location of the region of study with its poorly perceived career prospects means that attention is often focused on sustaining services, rather than expansion; many respondents with young children spoke of planning to move away to places with better services and prospects, meaning that a continuity and a sense of history are diminished.

Taken together, these factors highlight how these subterranean sacred spaces are the mark of a pioneer group. Operating in the context of a lack of precedence to build on, or without large numbers and political capital, the Islamic sacred spaces in west Wales have a subterranean ontology due to the particular context of Muslim settlement in that region. Their use of makeshift and contingent sacred spaces is a tactical response to a lack of purpose-built religious facilities in the region: using what is available to meet their devotional needs for the time-being. Other constraints, such as the short periods of residence and steady turnover, perpetuate this pioneer-like condition, leading to a fixed temporariness. Consequently, the use of these spaces perpetuates a visible absence from the lived landscape of west Wales.

Considering these spaces as spaces of pioneers gives valuable insight into the use and development of sacred spaces. Such a position not only acknowledges the active citizenship of local Muslims in acquiring these spaces, making-do with what is at hand and shaping the way in which it is used, but also the fragile contingency of such developments: they are reliant on negotiations with other actors, such as non-Muslim stakeholders, and are in an impermanent, unfinished state. This temporal attribute is particularly significant, as is shown in the development of the Old Gymnasium, for example, into a contingent sacred space. Despite its storefront nature, its physical presence and use for over 20 years allows it to function as a counter-public arena and more traces of Muslims' presence in west Wales are subsequently evident than with makeshift spaces such as empty rooms momentarily sacred through prayer. Had previous events turned out differently, the Old Gymnasium would itself have been replaced with a purpose-built facility on the university's campus. Hence, the absence is relative rather than absolute and illustrates a way in which Muslims in west Wales may become more present in future.

Conclusions

This paper has examined the ways that Muslims in west Wales negotiate aspects of absence and presence in their everyday lives. It has highlighted the juxtaposition between the visible absence and physical presence of Muslims and Islamic sacred spaces in rural west Wales. While these spaces do not acknowledge the presence of Muslims in the region, or attest to the actions that take place within them, they serve as important public arenas for those wishing to practise their faith and perform their religious identities. However, the visible absence undermines such spaces' public potential, as newcomers often express difficulty in finding these spaces and accessing their services. Characteristic of makeshift and contingent sacred spaces, they are invariably owned and controlled by other actors and their ability to serve as counter-public arenas is limited, as organisations may not have full access to these spaces or the ability to direct development aligned with their needs. Such a situation is consolidated by the particular dynamics of local Muslims' demographics, which make longer-term strategies difficult and sustaining existing services a priority. Consequently, Muslims rely on a tactical 'making-do' of facilities that often results in a 'fixed temporariness', as these makeshift and contingent spaces become longer-term solutions rather than shorter-term accommodations.

This paper has also highlighted two key implications for understanding multiculturalism in rural areas. First, it illustrates the active citizenship taken by members of minority groups to meet particular requirements, such as devotional needs. As Robinson and Gardner (2004) note, non-governmental organisations, charities and umbrella groups catering for minority interests have an urban clustering, meaning that rural inhabitants, who are more likely to face hate crimes, are less likely to have access to formal support organisations. As many religious services are not readily available for rural Muslims, they must rely on their own efforts and co-operation to develop and sustain them. For many respondents, the additional effort needed to access these services is something positive as it displays determination to fulfil religious duties, rather than through more passive forms of habit or convenience. Unlike their urban counterparts, rural Muslims cannot access such a comprehensive range of services and facilities; instead, they must choose those aspects that are most important, desirable or achievable, representing a calculated approach in the context of resources available.

Secondly, this paper has indicated that social cohesion is not only an urban phenomenon. Non-Muslim actors play significant roles in helping to provide makeshift and contingent sacred spaces. While some organisations may benefit from renting rooms or developing services to attract lucrative international students, there is also an element of goodwill in these actions that should not be overlooked. This can be seen as representing the sense of hospitality of a good employer in promoting inclusive workforces, particularly when these organis- ations attract a number of Muslim employees or students to the region. The enactment of social cohesion, and the particular role of workplaces in rural cohesion is worthy of further study.

The subterranean ontology invoked in this paper also has implications for the study of absence. The subterranean concept—which ought not to privilege clan- destine associations—is particularly useful in thinking of the juxtapositions of absence and presence, where something may be present in one sense, but absent in another. In this sense, its dual ontology contests absolutist conceptions that position bodies, discourses and acts as wholly present or wholly absent, by allowing these properties to co-exist. Indeed, the surface and sub-surface are co- constituted. In regard to infrastructure, the surface world is dependent on the sub- terranean. Traces of the subterranean can be seen on the surface world through drains, exposed pipes and skylights to cellars.

Visibility is central to the conception of the subterranean. The very distinction relies on the surface providing a barrier, limiting visual technology from seeing the underground, constructing it as unknown and secret (Perkins and Dodge, 2009). However, the rise of sophisticated sound-based mapping technology brings a realisation that this distinction is not universal, but centred on the hege- mony of vision. What is absent and what is present, as Robinson (this Special Issue) notes, is a question of gaze. The prevalent constructions of rural areas (as well as minority nations) as homogeneous communities where others are absent are particularly significant in reinforcing such a gaze. Consequently, there is a need to acknowledge and unpack the factors that construct such a gaze and prioritise particular perspectives and foci. Such a venture would destabilise the god-like position that is emphasised by vertical ontologies and would allow for alternative conceptions.

Acknowledgements

The research discussed in this paper was funded by the Council for Welsh- Medium Higher Education's postgraduate teaching scholarship (YSG0611). The author is grateful to Professor Mike Woods and two anonymous referees for their helpful comments, and for the editorial guidance of Professor Ronan Paddi- son.

Notes

1. The 2001 census included, for the first time, a voluntary question on religion. Consequently, the accuracy of the figures may be contested and they do not allow for comparisons until the 2011 figures are published.
2. The University of Wales, Lampeter and Trinity College, Carmarthen, merged in 2010 to form The University of Wales Trinity-St David's.
3. Bressey (2009) accounts for the presence of 'Black moors' and 'Saracens' in rural England in Wales throughout the 17th century. Given the descriptions, and the baptism records of many of these indi- viduals, it is likely that Muslims were also found in rural England and Wales at this time. While no explicit mention is made of west Wales in Bressey's study, it is feasible that Muslim Africans could have been found in this region at this time as many local landowners were involved in similar colonial and slavery projects.

4. While the Church of England remains the Established Church in England, it was disestablished in Wales in 1920, following the enactment of the Wales Church Act 1913; Wales and Northern Ireland are the only parts of the United Kingdom where secularism has a legal foundation. However, Wales' societal culture remains heavily influenced by Christian traditions, even though only 9 per cent of Wales' populace regularly attended a place of worship in 1995 (Chambers and Thompson, 2005).

5. Carmarthen Town Council had a Muslim Councillor between 2008 and 2012.

References

AMIN, A. (2002) Ethnicity and the multicultural city: living with diversity, *Environment and Planning A*, 34(6), pp. 959–980.

AMIN, A. (2004) Regions unbound: towards a new politics of place, *Geografiska Annaler*, 86B(1), pp. 33–44.

BAKER, C. and SKINNER, H. (2006) *Faith in action: the dynamic connection between spiritual and religious capital*. Manchester: The William Temple Foundation.

BEAUMONT, J. (2008a) Introduction: faith-based organisations and urban social issues, *Urban Studies*, 45(10), pp. 2011–2017.

BEAUMONT, J. (2008b) Faith action on urban social issues, *Urban Studies*, 45(10), pp. 2019–2034.

BECK, J. (2011) Signs of the sky, signs of the times: photography as double agent, *Theory, Culture & Society*, 28(7/8), pp. 123–139.

BISHOP, R. (2011) Project 'Transparent Earth' and the autoscopy of aerial targeting: the visual geopolitics of the underground, *Theory, Culture & Society*, 28(7/8), pp. 270–286.

BRESSEY, C. (2009) Cultural archaeology and historical geographies of the black presence in rural England, *Journal of Rural Studies*, 25(4), pp. 386–395.

BRICE, M. A. K. (2009) Residential integration: evidence from the UK census, in: R. PHILLIPS (Ed.) *Muslim Spaces of Hope: Geographies of Possibility in Britain and the West*, pp. 222–235. London: Zed Books.

BUGG, L. B. (2012) Religion on the fringe: the representation of space and minority religious facilities in the rural-urban fringe of metropolitan Sydney, Australia, *Australian Geographer*, 43(3), pp. 273–289.

CANTLE, T. (2004) *The End of Parallel Lives? The Report of the Community Cohesion Panel*. London: Home Office.

CASANOVA, J. (2005) Catholic and Muslim politics in comparative perspective, *Taiwan Journal of Democracy*, 1(2), pp. 89–108.

CERTEAU, M. DE (1984) *The Practice of Everyday Life*. Berkley, CA: University of California Press.

CHAMBERS, P. and THOMPSON, A. (2005) Coming to terms with the past: religion and identity in Wales, *Social Compass*, 52(2), pp. 337–352.

CRESSWELL, T. (1996) *In Place/Out of Place: Geography, Ideology, and Transgression*. Minneapolis, MN: University of Minneapolis Press.

DAFYDD JONES, R. (2010) Islam and the rural landscape: discourses of absence in west Wales, *Social and Cultural Geography*, 11(8), pp. 751–768.

DUNN, K. M. (2004) Islam in Sydney: contesting the discourse of absence, *Australian Geographer*, 35(3), pp. 333–353.

EADE, J. (1996) Nationalism, community and the islamization of space in London, in: B. D. METCALF (Ed.) *Making Muslim Space in North America and Europe*, pp. 217–233. Berkley, CA: University of California Press.

ELLIS, M., WRIGHT, R. and PARKS, V. (2004) Work together, live apart? Geographies of racial and ethnic segregation at home and at work, *Annals of the Association of American Geographers*, 94(3), pp. 620–637.

FRASER, N. (1990) Rethinking the public sphere: a contribution to the critique of actually existing democracy, *Social Text*, 25(1), pp. 56–80.

GARRETT, B. L. (2011) Cracking the Paris carrières: corporal terror and illicit encounter under the city of light, *ACME: An International e-Journal for Critical Geographies*, 10(2), pp. 269–277.

GILLIAT-RAY, S. and MELLOR, J. (2010) *Bilad al-Welsh* (the Land of the Welsh): Muslims in Cardiff, South Wales—past, present and future, *The Muslim World*, 100(4), pp. 452–475.

GRAY, D., FARINGTON, J., SHAW, J., MARTIN, S. and ROBERTS, D. (2001) Car dependence in rural Scotland: transport policy, devolution and the impact of the fuel duty escalator, *Journal of Rural Studies*, 17(1), pp. 113–125.

GRUFFUDD, P. (1994) Back to the land: historiography, rurality and the nation in interwar Wales, *Transactions of the Institute of British Geographers*, 19(1), pp. 61–77.

GRUFFUDD, P. (1995) Remaking Wales: nation-building and the geographical imagination, 1925–50, *Political Geography*, 14(3), pp. 219–239.

HOPKINS, P. (2006) Youthful Muslim masculinities: gender and generational relations, *Transactions of the Institute of British Geographers*, 31(3), pp. 337–352.

HOPKINS, P. (2011) Towards critical geographies of the university campus: understanding the contested experiences of Muslim students, *Transactions of the Institute of British Geographers*, 36(1), pp. 157–196.

IANNACCONE, L. R. (1990) Religious practice: a human capital approach, *Journal for the Scientific Study of Religion*, 29(3), pp. 297–314.

KONG, L. (2005) Religious landscapes, in: J. DUNCAN, N. JOHNSON and R. SCHEIN (Eds) *A Companion to Cultural Geography*, pp. 365–381. Oxford: Blackwell.

LEY, D. (2008) The immigrant church as an urban service hub, *Urban Studies*, 45(10), pp. 2057–2074.

MILBOURNE, P. and CLOKE, P. (2006) Introduction: the hidden faces of rural homelessness, in: P. MILBOURNE and P. CLOKE (Eds) *International Perspectives on Rural Homelessness*, pp. 1–8. London: Routledge.

MODOOD, T. (2006) British Muslims and the politics of multiculturalism, in: T. MODOOD, A. TRIANDAFYL-LIDOU and R. ZAPATA-BARRERO (Eds) *Multiculturalism, Muslims and Citizenship: A European Approach*, pp. 37–56. London: Routledge.

NAGEL, C. and STAEHELI, L. (2008) Integration and the negotiation of 'here' and 'there': the case of British Arab activists, *Social and Cultural Geography*, 9(4), pp. 415–430.

NAYLOR, S. and RYAN, J. R. (2002) The mosque in the suburbs: neogtiating religion and ethnicity in South London, *Social and Cultural Geography*, 3(1), pp. 39–59.

NAYLOR, S. and RYAN, J. R. (2003) Mosques, temples and gurdwaras: new sites of religion in twentieth-century Brita, in: D. GILBERT, D. MATLESS and B. SHORT (Eds) *Geographies of British Modernity: Space and Society in the Twentieth Century*, pp. 168–183. Oxford: Blackwell.

NEAL, S. (2002) Rural landscapes, representations and racism: examining multicultural citizenship and policy-making in the English countryside, *Ethnic and Racial Studies*, 25(3), pp. 442–461.

PAIN, R. and SMITH, S. (Eds). (2008) *Fear: Critical Geopolitics and Everyday Life*. Aldershot: Ashgate.

PEACH, C. (2006) Islam, ethnicity and South Asian religions in the London 2001 census, *Transactions of the Institute of British Geographers*, 31(3), pp. 353–370.

PERKINS, C. and DODGE, M. (2009) Satellite imagery and the spectacle of secret spaces, *Geoforum*, 40(4), pp. 546–560.

PHILLIPS, D. (2006) Parallel lives? Challenging discourses of British-Muslim self-segregation, *Environment & Planning D*, 24(1), pp. 25–40.

PIKE, D. (2005) The Walt Disney underground, *Space and Culture*, 8(1), pp. 47–65.

PUTNAM, R. D. (2000) *Bowling Alone: The Collapse and Revival of American Community*. London: Touchstone.

ROBINSON, J. (2012) Invisible targets, strengthened morale: static camouflage as a 'weapon of the weak', *Space & Policy*, 16(3), pp. 351–368.

ROBINSON, V. (2003) Exploring myths about rural racism: a Welsh case study, in: C. WILLIAMS, N. EVANS and P. O'LEARY (Eds) *A Tolerant Nation? Exploring ethnic diversity in Wales*, pp. 160–178. Cardiff: University of Wales Press.

ROBINSON, V. and GARDNER, H. (2004) Unravelling a stereotype: the lived experience of black and minority ethnic people in rural Wales, in: N. CHAKRABORTI and J. GARLAND (Eds) *Rural Racism*, pp. 85–107. Cullompton: Willan.

ROUTLEDGE, P. (2003) Convergence space: process geographies of grassroots globalization networks, *Transactions of the Institute of British Geographers*, 28(3), pp. 333–349.

SANGHERA, G. S. and THAPAR-BJÖKERT, S. (2008) Methodological dilemmas: gatekeepers and positionality in Bradford, *Ethnic and Racial Studies*, 31(3), pp. 543–562.

SCOTT, H. V. (2008) Colonialism, landscape and the subterranean, *Geography Compass*, 2(6), pp. 1853–1869.

SCOTT, J. C. (1985) *Weapons of the Weak: Everyday Forms of Peasant Resistance*. New Haven, CT: Yale University Press.

SCOTT, J. C. (1990) *Domination and the Arts of Resistance: Hidden Transcripts*. New Haven, CT: Yale University Press.

SLYMOVICS, S. (1996) The Muslim World Day Parade and 'Storefront' Mosques of New York City, in: B. D. METCALF (Ed.) *Making Muslim Space in North America and Europe*, pp. 204–216. Berkley, CA: University of California Press.

SOLOMON, T. (2005) 'Living underground is tough': authenticity and locality in the hip-hop community in Istanbul, Turkey, *Popular Music*, 24(1), pp. 1–20.

STAEHELI, L. A. (1996) Publicity, privacy, and women's political action, *Environment & Planning D*, 14(5), pp. 601–619.

STAEHELI, L. A. and MITCHELL, D. (2008) *The People's Property? Power, Politics and the Public*. London: Routledge.

VERTER, B. (2003) Spiritual capital: theorizing religion with Bourdieu against Bourdieu, *Sociological Theory*, 21(2), pp. 150–174.

WERBNER, P. (2000) Divided loyalties, empowered citizenship? Muslims in Britain, *Citizenship Studies*, 4(3), pp. 307–324.

WILLIAMS, R. (2008) *Notes on the Underground: An Essay on Technology, Society, and the Imagination*. Cambridge, MA: MIT Press.

Invisible Targets, Strengthened Morale: Static Camouflage as a 'Weapon of the Weak'

JAMES PHILIP ROBINSON

Abstract. In the natural world, camouflage is habitually deployed by 'vulnerable' creatures to deceive predators. Such protective strategies have been culturally, socially and technologically translated into human societies, whereby camouflage has been used to mask intentions, actions, feelings and valuable objects or spaces. Through the material presence of such techniques, everyday spaces can become inscribed as places of sanctuary. Focusing on British civil camouflage work of the 1930s and 1940s, this paper explores the historical, cultural and political connotations of camouflage and how the attainment of invisibility, as a 'weapon of the weak', can both physically and affectively protect urban populations.

Introduction

In the natural world, the act of camouflage is habitually deployed by a variety of creatures for a multitude of purposes. On the one hand, it is utilised offensively by predators as a means of approaching prey relatively undetected; the tiger, for example, "will approach prey low through foliage, camouflaged through disruptive-patterned stripes, cryptic colouration, and countershading" (Blechman and Newman, 2004, p. 80). In an attempt to reduce their vulnerability, hunted creatures may also resort to the adoption of one (or even a combination) of several forms of camouflage. This protection may take the form of 'mimetic resemblance', whereby the colours, patterns and forms of the surrounding environment or, in some cases, the behaviours and habits of other (more 'dangerous') species, may be simulated. Others may attempt 'obliterative shading' or 'countershading' in order to misguide the perceptive abilities of their predators; in the former, the 'hunted' attempts to break up its shape and form by 'dazzling' the predator, whereas in the latter, "the undersides of animals are lighter than the surfaces that have greater exposure to sunlight" (Behrens, 2009, p. 498), enabling 'merging' through tonal resemblance. Finally, creatures may also combine these techniques with other more-than-visual methods; cuttlefish, squid and octopi utilise ink as a screen, inhibiting sight and smell, whereas various species of moths are known to utilise 'radar camouflage' to confuse the bats which hunt them (Blechman and

Newman, 2004; Ruxton, 2011; for further works on 'biological' camouflage, see Stevens and Merilaita, 2011). Such tactics are integral to their continued survival, allowing 'threatened' species to carry out their daily routines by 'passively' (or in some cases, 'actively') deterring potential predators.

While this opening narrative testifies to the 'natural' and non-human deployment of camouflage, camouflage acts also play an intrinsic role in the everyday spaces and practices of the human world. In this paper, consideration is given to the nuanced ways in which camouflage, as a practice that entails the transition towards making someone or something materially or visually absent, has permeated and shaped everyday life. Building upon existing work which has examined how absence is deployed for social and political ends, from the masking of intentions, actions and feelings to the hiding of objects or spaces considered to be valuable, the paper highlights how camouflage (conceived here as an umbrella term that encompasses a wide range of descriptors: absence, hiddenness, concealment, dissimulation, effacement, etc.) possesses an inherently spatial dimension that needs to be explored. More specifically, it contends that, through the translation and extension of its protective and non-human operationalities into the human world, everyday spaces can become transformed into and re-inscribed as places of sanctuary, safety and security. Viewing camouflage as a 'weapon of the weak' (Scott, 1985, 1990) or a 'generative' tool that enables physical and psychological resistance through seemingly mundane or 'obscured' acts of 'active participation', complex relationships of and interplays between absence and presence come to the fore. Focusing on the British civil camouflage project conducted during the Second World War, the paper examines how the deployment of camouflage as a defensive technique was utilised to protect industrial installations deemed to be vital to the war effort. Devised to distract the attentions of the aerial bomber away from such manufacturing spaces, it is argued that the application of cunning designs and inventive methods served a dual purpose: to prevent physical destruction and disrupted production, as well as to boost the morale of a perceived-to-be civilian population.

The paper is structured into five sections. The first considers human appropriations and practices of camouflage, reflecting upon the heterogeneous ways in which it is, and has been, routinely present as part of everyday life. While scholarly and popular attention has predominantly focused upon its cultural and militaristic dimensions, this section outlines the need to consider more fully the highly politicised ways in which camouflage is often used as an everyday tactic and/or technology of resistance against the 'powerful' and the 'feared'. Following on from this, the second section examines the pervasive cultural and political imaginings of the 'aerial threat' in the 1930s, contextualising governmental fears about the breakdown of 'stoical endurance'. Positioned within a much broader framework of civil defence strategies, the third section examines the role of camouflage in managing civilian morale and explores the techniques and methods which were deployed to help protect Britain's industrial heartlands. The penultimate section then considers the perceived material and psychological effects that camouflage was seen to have upon the British workforce (and the populace more broadly), with its 'presence' enabling the reinforcement of national, regional and local solidarity, and, in contrast, its 'absence' being viewed as detrimental to both economic and social performance. The final section offers some concluding remarks about the complex entanglement of different conditions and practices of absence and presence which are inherent to its practice.

Camouflage and the Human World

While the practice of camouflage has been explored in evolutionary terms for non-human animals (Forbes, 2011), its presence in the human world has been conceived as a social, cultural and technological adaption and appropriation (Newark, 2007; Shell, 2012). Indeed, the translation of the epistemologies of 'natural' camouflage into the 'social' world has been extremely multifarious, with camouflage knowledges, practices and aesthetics being extended and transmuted into a variety of human activities, pursuits and endeavours. Hunters, from the prehistorical period through to the present-day, have and continue to utilise lessons learned from nature to remove their visual and olfactory 'presence' (Newark, 2007, pp. 48–51); artists have explored the historical relationship between art and camouflage and have drawn upon natural performances of camouflage to inform their own work (Atterbury, 1975; Behrens, 1987, 2002; Richardson, 1999; Newark, 2002); contemporary architectural discourses have embraced camouflage aesthetics to help facilitate the merging of new, physical structures into the landscape (Leach, 2006; Newark, 2007, pp. 186–189); even fashion, from cat-walk to high-street 'animal print' brands, bear traces of the cultural appropriation of camouflage (Blechman and Newman, 2004). Yet perhaps the most commonly recognised translation is in its militarised appropriation as a technology of war, most notably since the First World War, when it

> emerged … as an overarching set of [militarised] practices forged by a shifting collective of human and non-human actors united in the aim of circumventing aerial reconnaissance technologies (Shell, 2012, p. 21).

Certainly, with the rise of modern, technological warfare and its effects upon spatial relations, camouflage has now become part of the everyday working and living environment of performing and carrying-out war, with camouflage schemes being developed and deployed to cater for a variety of 'hostile' environments: woodland, deserts, snowscapes and the urban environment. Today, soldiers are provided with camouflage attire, wear camouflaged headgear and mask their faces with face-paint; even military hardware, from motorised vehicles and aeroplanes to guns and ships, is adorned in camouflage patterns that embody the natural techniques of mimicry, disruption and countershading (Newark *et al.*, 1996; Brayley, 2010).

While great academic and popular attention has been directed towards these cultural, aesthetical and militaristic appropriations of camouflage, several observations may be made. First, the political connotations of camouflage have been relatively underexplored and, where discussions of these political aspects have taken place, analyses have often been confined to the symbolic and iconographical power of camouflage patterning. Newark *et al.* (1996, p. 36), for example, have remarked upon the importance of camouflage as "a statement of national identity", noting how "each nation looks upon the creation of a camouflage suit as a step towards independence as important as creating its own flag". Moreover, they draw attention to the use of camouflage to *symbolise* resistance and militancy, observing how it has been worn by individuals associated with environmental activism and anti-war protesting. These accounts of camouflage as resistance, however, focus solely on camouflage as *representation*, rather than as an everyday political *practice*.

Inspired by recent engagements with more-than-representational theory with its emphasis upon practice (Lorimer, 2005; Thrift, 2007), combined with the work of James C. Scott, it is argued here that camouflage acts are a significant and important everyday practice that enables the resistance of the 'weak'. In his seminal work *Domination and the Arts of Resistance* (1990), Scott examines the 'arts of political disguise' deployed by the 'weak' to avoid any explicit display of insubordination for fear of repercussions from the 'powerful'. Utilising the empirical example of the Malayan peasantry, Scott emphasises how

> subordinate groups have developed a large arsenal of techniques that serve to shield their identity while facilitating open criticisms, threats and attacks. Prominent techniques that accomplish this purpose include spirit possession, gossip, aggression through magic, rumour, anonymous threats and violence, the anonymous letter and anonymous mass defiance (Scott, 1990, p. 140).

For him, these deceptive and concealed tactics act as everyday 'weapons of the weak' (Scott, 1985); they are 'everyday' in the sense that they are relatively passive, rather than explicitly open, acts of resistance, they are concerned with immediate rather than long-term effects and they "make no headlines" (Scott, 1990, pp. 33–36). Although such practices are rendered 'absent' both through the anonymity of their performance and through the subsequent lack of attention given to them by the 'powerful', their 'presence', nevertheless, acts as an effective means of inspiring confidence amongst the 'weak'. Building upon these assertions through the work of Arreguín-Toft (2005), camouflage practices can be envisaged as effective tools of resistance in 'asymmetric conflicts', enabling the 'weak to win wars'. In applying an 'opposite-approach', whereby the powerless use 'indirect and passive' techniques against the more 'direct and active' methods deployed by the powerful, Arreguín-Toft (2005, p. 24) contends that "weak actors are much more likely to win than the conventional wisdom allows for". For both Scott and Arreguín-Toft, it is the strategies and tactics which the 'weak' choose to deploy which have a bearing on the outcome. Embodying the 'protective' rationales that shape its role in the 'struggle for existence', the attainment of invisibility clearly acts as a political 'weapon of the weak' that enables the subverting of established hierarchical power relations in favour of the 'weak'. Moreover, through its ability to forge 'tough-mindedness', the material and psychological benefits of camouflage permit resistance movements to become united and strengthened.

A second observation to be made about these studies of camouflage is also the significant overlooking of the spatial dimensions and interactions involved in its practice. Although the relationship between absence, presence and space has been explored in a multitude of geographical-related contexts, from appreciations of landscape (Rose, 2006; Wylie, 2009) to 'spectro-geographies' (Maddern and Adey, 2008) and the effects of virtual technology in transforming conceptions of distance and proximity (Paterson, 2006), more focused and critical explorations of camouflage itself, as a spatial practice that encapsulates complex interplays of absence and presence, have been surprisingly absent (although increasingly, attempts are beginning to reflect upon this; see Forsyth, under review; Robinson, under review a, under review b). In reflecting upon some of the empirical examples already presented, it is clear that camouflage is an inherently spatial practice. At a very basic level, 'effective' camouflage is only obtainable through an attentiveness to surrounding conditions, actions and environments. It is through such considerations of the immediate vicinity that spaces, places and landscapes are transformed, not just materially, but also imaginatively and symbolically. In particular, camouflage's close association with 'nature' (and its social and cultural imaginings) has meant that social space has become imbued and rendered as an emotional space of sanctuary and refuge; such attributes are positioned alongside other everyday uses of these spaces (see Dafydd Jones, this Special Issue). Historical and culturally, the idea of 'nature' has frequently been evoked as a source of peace, solitude and of significant importance to the well-being of the human body (Matless, 1998; Edensor, 2001). Little (2008, p. 87), for example, highlights that while 'nature' can be envisaged as a highly complex concept, evoking different meanings and understandings, modern societies frequently resort to it as "a protector against fear ... providing security against an unpredictable human threat". Such conceptualisations have resulted in the demarcation of particular spaces as being of benefit to the human condition; this is particularly true of rural spaces, where, Little argues, 'nature' has emerged as a "buffer against fear, a protector of rural spaces and communities and as a counter to the evil influences of progress, modernity and the urban" (Little, 2008, p.90).

While rural spaces are considered to be sites where the 'natural' is most prominent, 'nature' also has a significant 'presence' in the modern city—namely, in the form of water, waste, food, commodities and energy (Kaika, 2005; Heynen *et al.*, 2005). However, this presence is usually an absent one; the infrastructural networks that sustain its presence are in effect 'invisible' to the everyday, only becoming 'present' as a result of 'catastrophic failure' or breakdown (Graham, 2006, p. 247; see also Star, 1999). Their vitality to the modern city has meant that such infrastructures have become targets of 'forced demodernisation' during times of political unrest, with

> both formal and informal political violence centr[ing] on the deliberate destruction, or manipulation, of the everyday urban infrastructures that are necessary to sustain the circulations and metabolisms of modern urban life. As urban life becomes ever more mediated by fixed, sunken infrastructures, so the forced denial of flow and circulation, becomes a powerful political and military weapon (Graham, 2006, p. 245).

With the evolution of 'the science[s] and practice[s] of destruction' over the course of the 20th century, and with it the increasing proliferation of 'zones of confrontation' between the technological and the corporeal (Bourke, 2006), these 'hidden' infrastructures have become increasingly present and therefore more easily targeted. The effect of this has been that the 'powerful' frequently resort to the destruction of these networks, rendering the 'powerless' unable to resist.

In the context of earlier discussions about the use of camouflage as resistance, the act of concealment in the city can be seen to play two fundamental roles. First, it is suggested that camouflage is not only an integral part of the everyday functioning of urban infrastructures, but provides a physical and psychological reassurance that those networks are functioning correctly. When such networks collapse and become present, panic of the populace materialises due to disrupted circulation and flow; in remaining visibly absent, such networks are known to be operating as 'normal' and thus everyday life is able to progress routinely. Secondly, camouflage may be considered by the 'powerless' to be an additional means of security; by making important infrastructures absent, camouflage acts subvert the capabilities of the 'powerful' to target those vital systems that sustain the city. Tapping into conceptions of nature as 'guardian' of the *status quo*, camouflage as a practice applied to the social world operates as a sort of "safe-guarding charm" and "magical protector" (Blechman and Newman, 2004, p. 685), rendering and demarcating spaces and places as sanctuaries and safe havens. As a 'weapon of the weak', the presence of camouflage acts within the urban landscape can be seen to subvert the gaze of the 'powerful', and enable the maintaining and strengthening of the resistive capabilities of the 'weak'.

The subsequent sections of this paper, therefore, consider the political and psychological implications of camouflage, particularly within an urban context, upon the abilities of the 'weak' to resist attack from the 'powerful'. With its emphasis upon the British civil camouflage project of the 1930s and 1940s, these sections position camouflage practices as one of several strategies devised to maintain the morale of a 'perceived-to-be' emotionally vulnerable population. In doing so, it suggested that such measures contributed to the task of conditioning Britons to resist the popular fears generated by the prospect of a comparatively weak (militarily, at least) nation-state at war against an enemy's technologically superior aerial force.

'Menace of the Clouds': Britain and the Emotional Cultures of the 'Aerial Threat'

> In future wars, great cities, such as London, will be attacked from the air ... for several days [it] will be one vast raving Bedlam, the hospitals will be stormed, traffic will cease, the homeless will shriek for help, the city will be in pandemonium. What of the government at Westminster? It will be swept away by an avalanche of terror. Then will the enemy dictate his terms, which will be grasped at like a straw by a drowning man ... war [may] be won in forty-eight hours (Fuller, 1923, p. 150).

Throughout the 1920s and 1930s, flying was beginning to emerge as 'the normal mode of travelling' (Adey *et al.*, 2007; Cwerner *et al.*, 2009), with notable developments in aeroplane technology being nurtured by the rapid expansion of commercial air travel and the fostering of 'airmindedness' within the national consciousness (Fearon, 1985). Going hand-in-hand with such developments, the aeroplane was celebrated for the ways in which it transformed the geographical imagination through enabling different ways of viewing and experiencing the world (Budd, 2010; McCormack, 2009; Millward, 2008; Simonsen, 2005). In this light, the aeroplane was very much cast as a 'technology of the future', as a 'winged gospel' (Corn, 1983).

Although these developments express the optimistic ways in which the aeroplane was embraced, these were eclipsed by the 'shadow of the bomber' (Bialer, 1980). Despite all its potentialities for future progress, its use and adaptability as a 'technology of war' struck great fear into the British populace, a fear premised upon and defined by the imagined and realised capabilities of the aeroplane to inflict significant material and psychological destruction on a scale captured in the narrative by Fuller quoted earlier. Such fears, however, had to emanate from somewhere, for

> fear does not pop out of the heavens and hover in the ether before blan-
> keting itself across huge segments of cities and societies; it has to be lived
> and made (Pain and Smith, 2008, p. 2).

So how did such anxieties about the aeroplane become articulated in the first place
and what were the affectual responses to this threat from the air?

In some respects, these fears emerged from the very 'materiality' of the air itself.
Due to the existence of very few natural obstacles, airspace was seen to allow an
aeroplane to strike with both speed and surprise; this ability to shock was considered by many contemporaries to be its most fear-inducing facet. In addition
to this, its ability to transcend the natural boundaries utilised on the ground to
demarcate territories and structure defence networks raised significant concerns
about the reach of aerial bombers to strike the industrial heartlands of Britain.
As Meilinger (1996, p. 247) writes, Britain had become used to being "sheltered
behind its moat for centuries", with this "protective shield" generating a "tradition of invulnerability". The aeroplane, however, was considered to destabilise
this tradition

> Britain [now] felt particularly vulnerable to air attack because the con-
> centration of political, financial, social and industrial power in the
> London area made it the most valuable target in the country. Worse,
> because it was so close to the Channel it was within easy striking
> range of air bases on the Continent (Meilinger, 1996, p. 261).

Finally, it was contended that the ability of the aeroplane to achieve 'vertical
depth' and a clear perspective of the world below not only rendered the industrial
landscape as increasingly present (and therefore targetable), but also served to
expose the 'collective affects' of the population such as morale (Anderson, 2010).

Interwar anxieties about the aerial threat, therefore, became centred on the fear
of the 'knock out' blow, with "anticipated damage and death on a scale compar-
able with what was, subsequently, feared from the use of atomic weapons"
(Campbell, 1982, p. 87). Such imaginings were evoked through a variety of
sources. Within popular media, the public were exposed to the visual experiences
of being attacked from the air in H. G. Wells' film *Things to Come* (1935) which
showed the destruction of 'Everytown' (modelled on London) (Wohl, 2005,
p. 217). The press also played a crucial role in the inciting of the 'Air Panic'. As
Holman notes, the press

> was for most people still the most important source of information about
> the wider world. Newsreels could not go into issues in any great depth,
> and radio did not come into its own until after the Sudeten crisis in 1938
> ... Only newspapers both reached a truly mass audience and provided
> both information and analysis (Holman, 2011, pp. 289–290).

Through 'interactive reading'—namely, through readers contributing letters to the
Editor—the public were able to express their own apprehensions, further exacer-
bating the growing paranoia.

Such imaginings and articulations of fear were further reinforced through
works produced by key aerial theorists such as P. R. C. Groves (a former British
representative on military aviation to the League of Nations), L. E. O. Charlton
and J. M. Spaight, amongst others, who were highly influential in exposing both
the dangers of an aerial attack and also the weaknesses in Britain's aerial

defence systems (Charlton, 1935, 1937; Groves, 1935; Spaight, 1938; Robinson, under review a). In addition to these accounts, the Royal Air Force were also aware of the effectiveness of aerial bombardment, with their own doctrine being centred around the targeting of particular strategic locations—namely, industrial sites and, where 'legitimate', worker populations to achieve particular 'effects'; for the RAF, "a nation was defeated when its people or government no longer retained the will to prosecute their war aim—the desired effect" (Meilinger, 2007, p. 142; see also Biddle, 2002; Smith, 1984; Jones, 1987). It was, therefore, predicted that anyone intent on attacking Britain would adopt similar tactics; visits by RAF officers to Germany in the first half of the 1930s (Orange, 2006), as well as the subsequent deployment of Luftwaffe aircraft during the Spanish Civil War (1936–39) confirmed such assumptions.

Following the rise to power of Adolf Hitler in 1933 and the gradual unravelling of the Versailles Treaty, these different imaginings and realities of a future air-based conflict defined Britain's foreign and defence policy. In attempting to resolve the situation, various political solutions were sought, with

> the Government persistently ... tr[ying] to secure international conventions which would provide for limitations on aircraft production, the abolition of the bomber, prohibitions of the act of bombing, a guarantee against air attack and a convention regulating the conduct of air warfare (Bialer, 1980, pp. 3–4).

Between 1932 and 1934, Britain's politicians were actively involved in the Geneva Disarmament Conference (Meilinger, 1999), as well as promoting the formation of an International Air Force to ensure collective security and disarmament (Holman, 2010), but both efforts came to no avail. As a result, many British politicians resigned themselves to accepting that "the only defence is in offence, which means that you have got to kill more women and children more quickly than the enemy if you want to save yourselves" (Baldwin, 1932); one simply had to break enemy morale before they broke yours. However, from 1935 such a strategy began to fall from favour following developments in radar technology which meant that

> the notion that bombers could strike virtually anywhere, at any time, from any direction, and achieve tactical surprise was no longer viable: bombers could be detected, intercepted, and stopped (Meilinger, 1996, p. 266).

With outdated biplanes expected to be inadequate against the new, fast mono-planes of the Luftwaffe, industrial output became geared towards constructing more effective fighters, such as the Hurricane and the Spitfire, rather than bombers, in order to meet parity with German production rates; such a shift reversed a trend which had been in existence since the mid 1920s. Despite this, aircraft production was still remarkably below that of the Luftwaffe, only surpassing it in 1940; it was clear that Britain needed more time to re-arm in order to face-off the Luftwaffe threat. While Prime Minister Neville Chamberlain's appeasement policy during this time-period has often been viewed as an attempt to avoid Britain being drawn into war, several revisionist historians have argued that appeasement was key to buying time for Britain to re-arm itself (Donnelly, 1999). It was against this backdrop that civil defence preparations began, with the object being to minimise the risk of fear spreading through the management of civilian morale, taken to mean the physical and psychological well-being of both the individual and collective society.

Civil Defence Planning and the Concealing of Britain's 'Home Front' Landscapes

Although a fighter force and radar technology would reduce the number of enemy aircraft reaching their targets, it was anticipated that some would still slip through, inflicting high levels of damage. In 1937, the Committee for Imperial Defence predicted that a 60-day offensive could kill as many as 600 000 and leave 1.2 million injured (Jones *et al.*, 2004, p. 465). While these figures caused much alarm, civil defence planners were more concerned about the breakdown of 'stoical endurance' that these raids would bring; three psychiatric casualties were to be expected for every physical one (Bourke, 2006, p. 228). When war broke out, it was contended that public morale would be tested to the limits, with individuals expected to suffer from the effects of lack of sleep, strain, 'war weariness' and potentially, 'freezing with fear'; even the queuing for food follow-ing an air raid was considered to lead potentially to outbreaks of mass panic (Summerfield, 1983). This susceptibility to fear was mapped onto both gender and class divisions. Women, in particular, were considered to be most susceptible, as were the working classes. Problems were also to be expected from the middle classes, who, it was argued, would be unco-operative and be more concerned with self-preservation. In some cases, even regional identity was evoked, with the 'North' being perceived as being more capable of enduring than the 'South', although some cities such as Southampton, which experienced heavy bombing, were considered as localised pockets of toughness (Beaven and Griffiths, 1999).

To counter the outbreak of fear, several tools of 'morale management' were devised, each focusing on key aspects which were believed to be of importance in sustaining morale. News concerning the war was to be regulated through censorship and the production of propaganda. Psychiatric clinics were set up on the outskirts of London to remove the emotionally fragile from society, whilst also seeking to 'cure' them of their trauma with patients still being able to hear bombs falling on the capital's centre (Jones *et al.*, 2004, p. 468). Various organis-ations were also employed to monitor morale levels across the country: Mass-Observation (founded by Tom Harrisson, Charles Madge and Humphrey Jennings in 1937), as well as intelligence branches in the Ministry of Information and Ministry of Home Security were all involved in the collection of information on the effects of bombing upon the British populace at large. Yet perhaps the most important measure to 'manage' morale was the Air Raid Precautions Department (ARPD), founded in 1935. Although an ARP Committee had been in operation as early as 1924, it was only following a meeting of the Defence Requirements Com-mittee in 1934 that a more centralised organisation was formed (O'Brien, 1955). Its role was to act as a "modulator of emotion" (Adey, 2010, p. 190) and was to concern itself "not [with] the protection of individuals and property from destruc-tion, but the 'maintenance of the morale of the people'" (Anon, 1937). As Adey (2010) has shown, ARP entailed preparing, controlling and regulating the body, physically and affectively, to contend with the aerial threat. Moreover, it enabled morale to be sustained through 'active participation' in defence, with individuals becoming responsible for their own and their neighbour's personal wellbeing; by putting the body 'to work', it was contended that a sense of hope could be articulated. People were, therefore, put in control of their own defence, albeit through guidance by a plethora of training literature (in 1938, every household received a copy of the manual *The Protection of Your Homes Against Air Raids*) or through their local ARP warden. This 'active participation' was deemed to be of the utmost importance in preventing the creeping-in of a 'deep shelter mentality', which, it was argued, could be extremely harmful to war-time production if the British populace chose to withdraw from society by hiding underground in air raid shelters (O'Brien, 1955, p. 1921; Jones *et al.*, 2006).

In addition to such measures as building air-raid shelters, the issuing of gas masks and evacuation, civil camouflage was also put forward as a solution for civil defence. It was imagined that civil camouflage could act as a 'passive' means of defence, supplementing not only these solutions, but also operating as part of a nationally integrated system of more 'offensive' modes of resistance composed of fighters, AA guns and radar. Commencing in October 1936, camouflage was to 'unsettle' the 'kill-chain' (Gregory, 2007), its purpose being to render an industrial installation 'absent' at particular "crucial moments" (Shell, 2012, p. 25). These "crucial moments" corresponded with particular 'events' during the course of the bombing run—namely, those points when the bomb-aimer/observer would be seeking to recognise and identify the presence of a key infrastructural site. In the case of civil camouflage work, a feature was to be rendered visually absent when examined from a distance of 3 miles at an altitude of 5000 ft, a set of operational parameters determined through considerations of bombing trajectories and the physiological capabilities of the human eye to discern and recognise targets at a distance from the air.

In November 1936, a list of 'typical' factories (virtually identical to the list of 'legitimate' targets identified by the RAF in the early 1920s) was circulated by the ARPD to the Camouflage Committee for consideration. On this list were features such as motor, aircraft and munitions factories, oil tank farms, gasometers, electricity generating stations, blast furnaces, waterworks and railway networks (Anon, 1936). Over the course of the next few years, this list was expanded into a much fuller catalogue of 'key points', with factories being included/excluded dependent upon their 'importance' as a target or aiming mark, their significance to war production and, drawing upon reports from the Air Warfare Analysis Section, statistical information as to the number of attacks committed in the local vicinity (Ministry of Home Security, 1945). Following identification of vulnerable sites, attempts would then be made at camouflage, with each establishment being viewed from the air by a Camouflage Officer; based at the Civil Defence Camouflage Establishment in Leamington Spa, this officer would be responsible for designing the scheme.

In terms of the camouflage strategies which were deployed, these were, in many ways, inspired by a combination of artistic, biological, scientific and engineering knowledges and practices (although it should be noted that frequent confrontations between the 'artist' school and the 'biological' school defined this period of camouflage work; see Forbes, 2011). It was through the utilisation of such knowledges that attempts would be made to address those attributes that rendered industrial features 'conspicuous' when viewed from the air; this included attending to contrasts in tone, colour, texture and form, as well as the presence of shadows that served to expose and 'make present' a building. In the vast majority of cases, paint-based solutions were often taken as the *de facto* response to the camouflage problem, an approach that achieved visual absencing through the combining of artistic and 'natural' principles in different ways. For example, *ARP Handbook No.11: Camouflage of Large Installations*, printed in February 1939, advocated painted schemes which made use of imitative and disruptive patterns (see Figure 1). Under imitation, it was advocated that a 'general pattern' simulating the local environment would be applied, enabling the industrial site to fit 'harmoniously' into its surroundings. In the context of urban areas, imitation usually took the form of the 'dwelling house' treatment, whereby the structure would be dressed up as terraced housing or a housing estate, with accompanying gardens and green spaces; such a technique was commonly used for factories with large roof expanses. In the case of disruption, described in the booklet as "a very successful form of animal camouflage", sharply contrasting colours and tones of paint would be utilised to break up the form and shape of the building; absence would, thus, be achieved through visual disorientation and disorder (Air Raid Precautions Department, 1939). In addition to these, simple toning down with a colour of middle or dark tone was also encouraged, with it being argued that such a scheme would facilitate the 'merging' of the structure into the landscape as well as aiding to reduce "visibility very considerably in dull light and also when looking down sun or moon" (Camouflage Committee, 1944).

However, the adoption of a solely paint-based approach was fraught with problems, not least through paint's inability to conceal cylindrical forms, such as gas holders and oil tanks, and to mask the presence of cast shadows. As a result, several alternative methods of rendering a building inconspicuous were also developed. Artificial netting was used to conceal shadows, to distort the shape and form of buildings as well as completely to hide features in the landscape. For such netting, careful selection of the garnishing materials was deemed essential, with it being remarked that the netting "had to conceal what was under the net and . . . [also] to show a surface which behaved optically like grass or whatever was appropriate to the general design" (Cave-Browne-Cave, 1945, p. 265). Such netting would, therefore, make use of materials such as coloured scrim (thin strips of hessian), sisal (a stiff fibre), steel wool, B. G. material (a sort of seaweed-based fibre) and chopped feathers in order to achieve this surficial similarity. Another technique was the use of texturing which, it was contended, "enhances greatly the value of a pattern not only by removing the danger of shine but also by endowing its colours with their proper tonal values under all

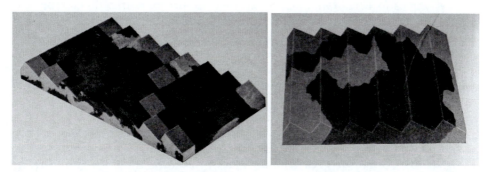

Figure 1. Models produced by the Camouflage Department to illustrate the application of imitation (*left*) and disruptive (*right*) paint patterns to buildings. *Source*: Air Raid Precautions Department (1939).

conditions of illumination" (Camouflage Committee, 1944); to attain this textural simulation, stone chippings, sand and grit, broken brick, wood chippings and cork granules would be applied to the vertical and horizontal surfaces of the building (Directorate of Camouflage, 1942). Through the adoption of one or several of these techniques, it was argued that effective concealment could be enacted to subvert the gaze of the bomber at those 'crucial moments' when the installation was being targeted.

Thinking through Effectiveness: the Material and Psychological Effects

The methods of camouflage which were used during this period were quite clearly eclectic, but the question is raised as to how effective they were as protection. In attempting to judge this effectiveness, attention can be drawn to two aspects—namely, its material and psychological benefits. The question of the physical protection that camouflage afforded was one that civil camoufleurs continuously sought answers to themselves, with judgements about 'success' being an integral part of the camouflaging process. Following the application of a camouflage scheme, visual assessments of the premises from the air were undertaken by the Camouflage Officer in order to ensure that the site would be rendered inconspicuous at the previously identified 'crucial moments'. If the scheme was 'satisfactory', it would be 'signed off'; if the results were disappointing, further recommendations would be made to bring it 'up-to-standard'. This observing of camouflaged features from the air ensured that visual absence, and therefore physical protection, could be guaranteed.

However, the far greater value of camouflage was the psychological protection that it was seen to afford. While primarily envisaged as a 'passive' technology of defence, civil camouflage was a practice that demanded 'active participation'. In the first instance, it required owners of industrial premises to mobilise individuals from the local community to enable the scheme to be applied; in seeking tenders for the work to be done, the Camouflage Directorate encouraged owners to employ local contractors and, as a by-product, reassure the local populace that something was being done to protect them. But 'home-front' camouflage also encouraged participation in other ways. Earlier in this paper, the significance of the press in enabling 'interactive reading' through correspondence to Editors was highlighted. Prior to 1941, when news on civil camouflage suddenly became censored, discussions on camouflage within newspapers were commonplace with contributors writing in with their own ideas about how to camouflage. In *The Times*, a great deal of enthusiasm was expressed for the use of 'car camouflage' by car owners, with it being noted that it "cost only a few shillings; [and] there are firms ready to undertake it ... Three colours are usually advised—light brown, medium green, and black" (*The Times*, 1940a). Later, such suggestions were retracted: "owners should not paint their cars with what is generally known as disruptive camouflage or with a jazz pattern. Cars painted in this way may be mistaken for Service vehicles, especially in poor light" (*The Times*, 1940b). In addition to these letters, the Camouflage Directorate itself also received correspondence from the public, identifying features which they considered to be 'conspicuous' as well as providing ideas about possible methods. For example, a letter was received from Mr Silver from Haslemere, Surrey, in which he wrote

> We have in our possession an open-air swimming pool, tiled in rather light blue, and I am wondering if I might ask your advice as to whether or not the presence of this pool is likely to constitute a danger by forming a landmark which might be of use to the Enemy ... in your opinion, would it be wise to empty the pool and cover it with bracken (Silver, 1940).

While this particular feature was deemed not to be dangerous, this example represents one of several cases where the British populace sought to become actively involved in its own defence.

Combined with 'active participation', it is clear that the mere presence of camouflage, as with other civil defence measures, could play a key role in maintaining and boosting morale, particularly in the unstable environment of the workplace. Previous practices of 'dazzle camouflage', applied to ships during the First World War, had shown the ability of the 'art of concealment' to captivate the public imagination and, in some respects, distract their attentions from the war (Atterbury, 1975; Williams, 2001). It was, therefore, maintained that camouflage could once again be used to aid 'the relaxation of the public'. With the commencing of the project, many early examples of civil camouflage were seen in this way. One example was Freeman's Meadow power station, located near Leicester, which appeared within both *The Times* and the journal *Popular Science* in December 1939 (see Figure 2). Painted with large trees on their sides, the towers were described as

> a mammoth Hollywood outdoor movie set, the vase-shaped cooling towers have a strange and fantastic appearance when viewed close-up ... but seen from a distance, it is said, the group is exceptionally hard to identify as the towers of a power plant (Anon, 1939a).

Although high regard was held for such schemes of this nature by the wider public, the ignorance of basic aesthetical principles such as perspective unsettled many of those working within official camouflage circles, who deemed such designs as 'dangerous' when viewed under 'operational' conditions. While such schemes may not have rendered the feature visually absent, their mere presence, nevertheless, seemed enough to foster the belief that protection was being afforded to workers.

Conversely, the absence of camouflage was considered by civil defence planners to undermine confidence in the government to protect its citizens. At the second meeting of the Camouflage Advisory Panel on 3 November 1939, the decision was taken not to use camouflage in London on account of the "configuration of [the] coastline [and] river banks [of the Thames] present[ing] landmarks impossible to conceal" (Anon, 1939b). This policy had profound implications on the concealment of some vital locations within the London area, most notably the oil farms at Thameshaven and Shellhaven. Due to it being argued that their location was well-known to enemy observers, the decision was taken not to spend the £25 000 (equivalent to £718 000 today) on camouflage. However, in the summer of 1940, while it was "fully accepted that camouflaging these tanks would not add to the safety of the tanks or of the district", Mr Lloyd of the Petroleum Department contended that

> the effects on morale of these not being camouflaged is considerable. The issue therefore turns on whether, from the point of view of the morale of

Camouflage Hides Power-Plant Towers

HUGE cooling towers that form a part of an electric generating plant at Freemen's Meadow, near Leicester, England, have been ingeniously camouflaged recently as a protection against the bombing planes of raiding enemy air fleets. Painted like stage scenery, or a mammoth Hollywood outdoor movie set, the vase-shaped cooling towers have a strange and fantastic appearance when viewed close-up, as in the photograph reproduced above, but seen from a distance, it is said, the group is exceptionally hard to identify as the towers of a power plant.

Figure 2. Freeman's Meadow electric generating plant, as it appeared in *Popular Science* (December 1939).

> those living and working in the area, it is desirable to have the oil tanks camouflaged (Lloyd, 1940).

In response, one camoufleur wrote that "I am bound to say that so long as bombs fall in the vicinity of the uncamouflaged tanks, the inhabitants will inevitably ascribe their danger to Government shortsightedness" (Galpin, 1940). Later on in the conflict, the ability of concealment strategies to strengthen public resolve was seen to bolster the cause of the civil camouflage project. In 1942, limitations were increasingly being placed upon both labour resources and available materials, putting camouflage work under tight constraints. In order to ensure the maintenance of the camouflage project, the Camouflage Directorate cited at least 20 cases where the presence of camouflage was seen to possess morale-boosting effects and influence productivity. In one report, it was noted how the owners of Fords at Dagenham "wrote a letter to the effect that they and their workers put down their immunity from any serious bomb damage to the camouflage and kept constantly maintaining it". Elsewhere, the presence of uncamouflaged features in close proximity to concealed structures was seen to evoke feelings of anxiousness; the occupiers of the Folland Aircraft factory at Southampton "wrote several times to express the serious concern of their employees that adjoining White air-raid shelters on a housing estate invalidated their camouflage scheme". The Bristol Aeroplane Company also reported workers getting 'restless' as a result of fading camouflage, resulting in calls for the scheme to be re-applied there (Anon, 1942). It is instances such as these that suggest that camouflage can be very much envisaged as an available 'weapon of the weak', enabling the material and psychological resistance of the 'powerless' through the presence of absence.

Conclusions

This paper has sought to unearth the political and symbolic connotations that the use of camouflage has in transforming the capabilities of the 'weak' to resist the 'powerful'. Indeed, it has been conceptualised as being integral to everyday encounters and political practices of resistance. As a practice, it operates as a 'weapon of the weak', a tool and a tactic drawn upon to enhance both the real and affective capacity to survive, resist and overcome the fears and asymmetric power relations that the 'weak' are exposed to through the ever-increasing proliferation of zones of confrontation with the 'powerful', zones produced through both technological advances and increased social mobility. While camouflage may hold its origins in the natural world, this paper has shown how the biological uses of camouflage have become significantly extended practically, aesthetically and imaginatively; camouflage and deception, as both *representation* and *practice*, now play a substantial role in shaping social and political clashes between the 'weak' and the 'powerful' in a variety of spatial contexts. Certainly, camouflage as a practice of absencing that seeks to create absence has profound implications upon the ways in which spaces, places and landscapes have become known, utilised and contested; they become re-inscribed and imbued with new meanings, demarcated as spaces of sanctuary, preservation and refuge from the 'powerful'. In the context of the modern city, camouflage has now become integral to its economic and social performance, with its everyday functioning asserting that the city is operating correctly and effectively. Furthermore, its presence is seen to enhance greatly the securitisation (both physically and imaginatively) of key infrastructural networks that sustain the city against both formal and informal acts of political aggression and violence.

In relation to the questions and agendas proposed by this Special Issue, this study of camouflage has demonstrated that concealment and deceptive acts produce rather interesting interplays, paradoxes and conflicts in terms of conceptualising absence and presence. On the one hand, this paper has demonstrated camouflage to be a practice that makes spaces appear absent at particular 'crucial moments'; for instance, when viewed by an observer under particular visual, temporal and spatial conditions, a camouflaged building becomes visually absent, while remaining physically present at the same time. Moreover, while camouflage is clearly a tactic which embodies the values of absence, it is nevertheless a technology which holds its value for the 'weak' by being both absent *and* present. As part of the fabric of everyday life, the presence of absence, in the form of camouflage, inspires confidence and assurance amongst the weak through the naturalisation of absence as normal. However, it is clear that, in order to benefit from this, one has to be cast as an 'insider' situated within and amongst its range of operationality. In other words, it is a practice whose presence is allowed to be known by some, but not by others; in this sense, it subverts established power relations, permitting the 'weak' to become the 'power-holders'. At the same time, absence of absence can be disconcerting; amongst the 'weak', it quickly becomes a matter for concern and anxiousness, producing disheartening effects. What camouflage seemingly possesses, therefore, is a powerful emotive value, enabled through its *situated presence* rather than *total absence*. This situatedness of presence and absence leads to further questions about both the explicit and more nuanced power relations built into the performance of certain camouflage acts, something which needs to be explored in future work. Such work should also consider the wider contexts of such performances, drawing attention to the more varied operationalities of camouflage, as both visual and non-visual technique, beyond that of simple protection. Finally, the effects of such practices upon how spaces are transformed materially and imaginatively also require consideration, with it being recognised that camouflage acts are not simply accepted wholeheartedly by everyone; they become grounds for contestation between different social and political groups and, ultimately, this has an effect upon the form that human landscapes may take. In light of these future research agendas, it is clear that the study of camouflage will be far from an absent presence; instead, it looks set to lead to the greater presence of absencing.

References

ADEY, P. (2010) *Aerial Life: Spaces, Mobilities, Affects*. Oxford: Blackwell.

ADEY, P., BUDD, L. and HUBBARD, P. (2007) Flying lessons: exploring the social and cultural geographies of global air travel, *Progress in Human Geography*, 31(6), pp. 773–791.

AIR RAID PRECAUTIONS DEPARTMENT (1939) *ARP Handbook No.11: Camouflage of Large Installations*. London: HMSO.

ANDERSON, B. (2010) Morale and the affective geographies of the 'war on terror', *Cultural Geographies*, 17(2), pp. 219–236.

ANON (1936) *CAM 7: list of typical examples of factories, 19th November 1936*. The National Archives (TNA), CAB17/170.

ANON (1937) *Minutes and report of the Warren Fisher Sub-committee of the CID on ARP Services, 30 June 1937*. TNA, CAB16/72.

ANON (1939a) Camouflage hides power-plant towers, *Popular Science*, 135(6), p. 129.

ANON (1939b) *Minutes of the second meeting of Camouflage Advisory Panel held on 3 November 1939*. TNA, HO186/171.

ANON (1942) *Untitled memorandum to the Director of Camouflage, 21 December*. TNA, HO186/1982.

ARREGUÍN-TOFT, I. (2005) *How the Weak Win Wars: A Theory of Asymmetric Conflict*. Cambridge: Cambridge University Press.

ATTERBURY, P. (1975) Dazzle painting in the First World War, *Antique Collector*, 46, pp. 25–29.

BALDWIN, S. (1932) The bomber will always get through, *The Times*, 11 November, p. 3.

BEAVEN, B. and GRIFFITHS, J. (1999) The blitz, civilian morale and the city: mass-observation and working class culture in Britain, 1940–1941, *Urban History*, 26(1), pp. 71–88.

BEHRENS, R. R. (1987) The art of dazzle painting, *Defence Analysis*, 3(3), pp. 233–243.

BEHRENS, R. R. (2002) *False Colors: Art, Design and Modern Camouflage*. Dysart, IA: Bobolink.

BEHRENS, R. R. (2009) Revisiting Abbott Thayer: non-scientific reflections about camouflage in art, war and zoology, *Philosophical Transactions of the Royal Society B*, 364(1516), pp. 497–501.

BIALER, U. (1980) *The shadow of the bomber: the fear of air attack and British politics, 1932–1939*. Royal Historical Society, London.

BIDDLE, T. D. (2002) *Rhetoric and Reality in Air Warfare: The Evolution of British and American Ideas about Strategic Bombing, 1914–1945*. Oxford: Princeton University Press.

BLECHMAN, H. and NEWMAN, A. (2004) *DPM—Disruptive Pattern Material: An Encyclopaedia of Camouflage: Nature, Military, Culture*. London: DPM Ltd.

BOURKE, J. (2006) *Fear: A Cultural History*. London: Virago.

BRAYLEY, M. J. (2010) *Camouflage Uniforms: International Combat Dress 1940–2010*. Marlborough: Crowood Press.

BUDD, L. (2010) On being aeromobile: airline passengers and the affective experiences of flight, *Journal of Transport Geography*, 19(5), pp. 1010–1016.

CAMOUFLAGE COMMITTEE (1944) *The principles and organization of static camouflage*. TNA, WORK28/11/8.

CAMPBELL, D. (1982) *War Plan UK: The Truth about Civil Defence in Britain*. London: Burnett Books.

CAVE-BROWNE-CAVE, T. R. (1945) Camouflage for the protection of civil factories and its application to peace-time purposes, *Journal of the Royal Society of Arts*, 93(4690), pp. 260–275.

CHARLTON, L. E. O. (1935) *War from the Air*. London: T. Nelson and Sons.

CHARLTON, L. E. O. (1937) *The Menace of the Clouds*. London: W. Hodge and Co.

CORN, J. J. (1983) *The Winged Gospel: America's Romance with Aviation*. Oxford: Oxford University Press.

CWERNER, S., KESSELRING, S. and URRY, J. (Eds). (2009) *Aeromobilities*. London: Routledge.

DIRECTORATE OF CAMOUFLAGE (1942) *Handbook of camouflage practice*. TNA, H0217/1.

DONNELLY, M. (1999) *Britain in the Second World War*. London: Routledge.

EDENSOR, T. (2001) Walking in the British countryside: reflexivity, embodied practices and ways of escape, in: P. MCNAUGHTEN and J. URRY (Eds) *Bodies of Nature*, pp. 81–106. London: Sage.

FEARON, P. (1985) The growth of aviation in Britain, *Journal of Contemporary History*, 20(1), pp. 21–40.

FORBES, P. (2011) *Dazzled and Deceived: Mimicry and Camouflage*. London: Yale University Press.

FORSYTH, I. (under review) Signatures in sand: geographies of the desert as theatre of war, *Environment and Planning A*.

FULLER, J. F. C. (1923) *The Reformation of War*. New York: Hutchinson.

GALPIN, C. J. (1940) *Memorandum to F. C. Johnson*. 16 July, TNA. HO186/1331.

GRAHAM, S. (2006) Urban metabolism as target: contemporary war as forced demodernization, in: N. HEYNEN, M. KAIKA and E. SWYNGEDOUW (Eds) *In the Nature of Cities: Urban Political Ecology and the Politics of Urban Metabolism*, pp. 245–265. London: Routledge.

GREGORY, D. (2007) In another time-zone, the bombs fall unsafely...: targets, civilians and late modern war, *Arab World Geographer*, 9(2), pp. 88–112.

GROVES, P. R. C. (1935) *Our Future in the Air*. London: Hutchinson.

HEYNEN, N., KAIKA, M. and SWYNGEDOUW, E. (Eds). (2005) *In the Nature of Cities: Urban Political Ecology and the Politics of Urban Metabolism*. London: Routledge.

HOLMAN, B. (2010) World police for world peace: British internationalism and the threat of a knock-out blow from the air, 1919–1945, *War in History*, 17(3), pp. 313–332.

HOLMAN, B. (2011) The air panic of 1935: British press opinion between disarmament and rearmament, *Journal of Contemporary History*, 46(2), pp. 288–307.

JONES, E., WOOLVEN, R., DURODIÉ, B. and WESSELY, S. (2004) Civilian morale during the Second World War: responses to air raids re-examined, *Social History of Medicine*, 17(3), pp. 463–479.

JONES, E., WOOLVEN, R., DURODIÉ, B. and WESSELY, S. (2006) Public panic and morale: Second World War civilian responses re-examined in the light of the current anti-terrorist campaign, *Journal of Risk Research*, 9(1), pp. 57–73.

JONES, N. (1987) *The Beginnings of Strategic Air Power: A History of the British Bombing Force, 1923–1939*. London: Frank Cass.

KAIKA, M. (2005) *City of Flows: Modernity, Nature, and the City*. London: Routledge.

LEACH, N. (2006) *Camouflage*. Cambridge, MA: MIT Press.

LITTLE, J. (2008) Nature, fear and rurality, in: R. PAIN and S. J. SMITH (Eds) *Fear: Critical Geopolitics and Everyday Life*, pp. 87–98. Aldershot: Ashgate.

LLOYD, G. (1940) *Letter to John Anderson, Minister of Home Security*. 9 July. TNA, HO186/1331.

LORIMER, H. (2005) Cultural geography: the busyness of being 'more-than-representational', *Progress in Human Geography*, 29(1), pp. 83–94.

MADDERN, J. and ADEY, P. (2008) Editorial: spectro-geographies, *Cultural Geographies*, 15(3), pp. 291–295.

MATLESS, D. (1998) *Landscape and Englishness*. London: Reaktion.

MCCORMACK, D. (2009) Aerostatic spacing: on things becoming lighter than air, *Transactions of the Institute of British Geographers*, 34(1), pp. 25–41.

MEILINGER, P. S. (1996) Trenchard and 'morale bombing': the evolution of Royal Air Force doctrine before World War Two, *The Journal of Military History*, 60(2), pp. 243–270.

MEILINGER, P. S. (1999) Clipping the bomber's wings: the Geneva disarmament conference and the Royal Air Force, 1932–1934, *War in History*, 6(3), pp. 306–330.

MEILINGER, P. S. (2007) A history of effects-based warfare, *The Journal of Military History*, 71(1), pp. 139–167.

MILLWARD, L. (2008) The embodied aerial subject: gendered mobility in British interwar air tours, *Journal of Transport History*, 29(1), pp. 5–22.

MINISTRY OF HOME SECURITY (1945) *Camouflage of Vital Factories and Key Points, 1939–1945*. TNA, HO191/3 .

NEWARK, T. (2002) *The Future of Camouflage*. London: No Nonsense Books.

NEWARK, T. (2007) *Camouflage*. London: Thames and Hudson.

NEWARK, T., NEWARK, Q. and BORSARELLO, J. F. (1996) *Brassey's Book of Camouflage*. London: Brassey.

O'BRIEN, T. (1955) *Civil Defence*. London: Longmans.

ORANGE, V. (2006) The German air force is already "the most powerful in Europe": two Royal Air Force officers report on a visit to Germany, 6–15 October 1936, *Journal of Military History*, 70(4), pp. 1011–1028.

PAIN, R. and SMITH, S. J. (2008) Fear: geopolitics and everyday life, in: R. PAIN and S. J. SMITH (Eds) *Fear: Critical Geopolitics and Everyday Life*, pp. 1–24. Aldershot: Ashgate.

PATERSON, M. (2006) Feel the presence: technologies of touch and distance, *Environment and Planning D*, 24(5), pp. 691–708.

RICHARDSON, B (1999) *Andy Warhol: Camouflage*. New York: Gagosian Gallery.

ROBINSON, J. (under review a) 'Concealing the crude': airmindedness and the camouflaging of Britain's oil installations, 1936–1939, in: P. ADEY, M. WHITEHEAD and A. WILLIAMS (Eds) *From Above: The Politics and Practice of the View from the Skies*. London: Hurst.

ROBINSON, J. (under review b) 'Darkened surfaces': camouflage and the nocturnal observation of Britain, 1941–1945, *Environment and Planning A*.

ROSE, M. (2006) Gathering 'dreams of presence': a project for the cultural landscape, *Environment and Planning D*, 24(4), pp. 537–554.

RUXTON, G. D. (2011) Evidence for camouflage involving senses other than vision, in: M. STEVENS and S. MERILAITA (Eds) *Animal Camouflage: Mechanisms and Functions*. Cambridge: Cambridge University Press.

SCOTT, J. C. (1985) *Weapons of the Weak: Everyday Forms of Resistance*. London: Yale University Press.

SCOTT, J. C. (1990) *Domination and the Arts of Resistance*. London: Yale University Press.

SHELL, H. R. (2012) *Hide and Seek: Camouflage, Photography and the Media of Reconnaissance*. New York: Zone Books.

SILVER, L. E. A. (1940) *Letter to the Air Minister*. 3 July. TNA, AIR2/2081.

SIMONSEN, D. G. (2005) Accelerating modernity: time–space compression in the wake of the aeroplane, *The Journal of Transport History*, 26(2), pp. 95–117.

SMITH, M. (1984) *British Air Strategy Between the Wars*. Oxford: Clarendon Press.

SPAIGHT, J. M. (1938) *Air Power in the Next War*. London: G. Bles.

STAR, S. (1999) The ethnography of infrastructure, *American Behavioural Scientist*, 43(3), pp. 377–391.

STEVENS, M. and MERILAITA, S. (Eds). (2011) *Animal Camouflage: Mechanisms and Functions*. Cambridge: Cambridge University Press.

SUMMERFIELD, P. (1983) Women, work and welfare: a study of child care and shopping in Britain in the Second World War, *Journal of Social History*, 17(2), pp. 249–269.

The Times (1940a) Camouflage for cars, 27 July, p. 6.

The Times (1940b) Camouflage of road vehicles, 26 August, p. 6.

THRIFT, N. (2007) *Non-representational Theory: Space, Politics, Affect*. London: Routledge.

WILLIAMS, D. (2001) *Naval Camouflage, 1914–1945*. London: Chatham Publishing.

WOHL, R. (2005) *The Spectacle of Flight: Aviation and the Western Imagination, 1920–1950*. London: Yale University Press.

WYLIE, J. (2009) Landscape, absence and the geographies of love, *Transactions of the Institute of British Geographers*, 34(3), pp. 275–289.

Index

INDEX

INDEX

INDEX